*How to Be
Faithful to Your
God-Given Mission*

THE CALL OF A LIFETIME

How to Be
Faithful to Your
God-Given Mission

THE
CALL OF A
LIFETIME

MICHAEL YOUSSEF

MOODY PRESS
CHICAGO

© 1996 by
MICHAEL YOUSSEF

ISBN: 0-8024-4190-4

1 3 5 7 9 10 8 6 4 2

Printed in the United States of America

*To my accountability partners,
who always speak the truth in love,
with deep gratitude and thanksgiving
to God for each one of you*

CONTENTS

INTRODUCTION
The Call to Membership in God's Corporation

I f you want to make it in this firm," said the senior partner, "you'll get in step with the rest of us."

The bewildered new lawyer had no idea what the head of the prestigious law firm meant, so he hurriedly mumbled, "I will, sir. Except, I'm not sure—"

"To start with," the executive cut in, immediately sensing the unasked question, "remove the family pictures from your desk. They tend to distract you from business."

"Yes, sir. I'll do that—"

"Oh, and something else . . . " The head of the firm paused, then ran down the list of what he called "small but significant" items—including the style of ties, the cut of suits, and in particular the importance of wearing highly polished black shoes with the laces carefully tied.

The young lawyer forced a smile onto his face as he noted each of these commandments.

"Just one more thing," his boss added. "I want you to know that half a day in this firm is just that—half a day—twelve hours. If you want to rise to the top, you must put in *more* than half a day's work!"

Before he turned to leave, he gave the young man a military salute and said, "Welcome aboard."

The moment the door closed, the young man sank back into his chair, suddenly aware that he was perspiring. *Is this what I've let myself in for?* he thought. Then he got a grip on himself, sat up, and said firmly, "OK! I'm going to show him I can do it. He's going to get the best and most hardworking lawyer he's ever had!"

BOTTOM-LINE BLUES

This is a true story. Does it sound extreme? Not for some firms. Especially not when they have top corporations on their roster and attract the hottest talent in the field. Such organizations know how alluring they are to the ambitious. They also know that if anyone wants to bail out there are twenty more applicants lining up at the door. When challenged, the corporate leaders reply with clichés:

"This is a dog-eat-dog world."
"We do what we have to do."
"You have to work fifteen hours a day just to stay even."
"The business of business is business."

And, most typically,

"The bottom line is beating the competition. Beating the competition translates into one word: profit."

Now, I'm not against bottom lines. Good businesses are profitable businesses. But the phrase is reductionistic. It no longer carries only its original meaning of "the figure below which a company operation ceases to be viable." It embodies a whole worldview, and every other priority must be sacrificed in the effort to keep the bottom line from being harmed. Money becomes the focus of attention. The assumption is that, whatever else you may want out of life, it comes by working as hard as is necessary to secure the maximum amount of revenue.

Anyone who, like the young lawyer, has just joined a powerful corporation is likely to see himself or herself standing at the foot of a long ladder, at the top of which lies the executive suite with its private washroom and access to elite dining facilities. It will take all their strength to climb that far. And, of course, the corporate ethos discourages distractions. The climbers don't talk about "ethics" or "morals"; they talk instead about "challenges" and "opportunities." They ask what they have to do to win, not whether such-and-such a strategy is moral. Ethics are for Sunday school, and lunch is for losers. The result is that businesspeople don't get out of life what they want and need. Let me give you an example.

When the crisis broke out over Iraq's invasion of Kuwait, almost immediately the media informed us that hundreds of Americans couldn't leave. A distraught wife in Texas told reporters that having her husband working in Kuwait meant "a new fishing boat, a new house trailer, and money for a secure retirement." She wailed, "John's not an adventurer. He went there for us."

> ### *Americans are tyrannized*
> ### *by the doctrine of the bottom line.*

I don't know the details. But the news clip left me with the impression that this lady, through no fault of her own, had bought the entire "bottom line" dream. Her husband was away from home. His kids were growing up without a father's daily influence. His wife had to cope with the twin burdens of a double parenting role and her own loneliness. Yet, in spite of that, she felt compelled to tell the waiting world, "I can't complain because he's working so hard . . . giving so much . . . and he's doing it all for us."

That family saw money—the bottom line—as the door to paradise. The husband gave his job everything because he thought it was the way to benefit his family. His family was expected to feel grateful that he was making the sacrifice. But in the end nobody got what they really wanted and needed: a husband, a wife, a father, children. They served the bottom line, and in return they got bottom-line lives— lives lived just above the threshold of viability.

Is This the American Way?

I believe that bottom-line thinking violates the principles of the American way of life, capitalism, and freedom, not to mention the Bible. Quite a few writers have been drawing attention to this. Rich DeVos of Amway Corporation recalls how, after his presentation to a college class, a professor argued, "Capitalists succeed because they aren't compassionate." DeVos replied, "Without capitalism there can be no compassion."

He's right. The problem isn't capitalism as a way of generating wealth. The problem lies in the fallacy that the bottom line is essential to preserve everything we hold dear. Make no mistake: it *is* a fallacy. There is no use pretending that the bottom line underpins the American way of life. It patently does not. Nor can we pretend that the competitiveness of American business depends on tax avoidance, extortionate relations with suppliers, attacks on whistle-blowers, or blind allegiance to company policy. Business doesn't *have* to operate that way. Yet from coast to coast Americans are tyrannized by the doctrine of the bottom line.

What concerns me most is how bottom-line thinking has spread not just through the business world but into politics, psychology, and even the church. Everywhere the positive values of goal-orientation, vision, achievement, and hard work are muddled with the idea that the only objectives worth aiming for are power, prestige, and possessions. Our priorities are in a mess. Yet Christians, more than anyone else, should be taking the lead and showing a better way.

I've Been There

I've been on the fast track. I was born in Egypt, a country where few of us had the breaks that average American kids take for granted. Later, when I came to America as an adult immigrant, I worked hard. Rewards came my way, and people recognized my talent and my commitment to produce.

In just four years I earned a Ph.D. from a prestigious

university, wrote three books, and became executive vice president of a Christian organization with worldwide offices. This position involved travel to dozens of countries, mostly in the Third World, all of it in service to God.

In the following four years, beginning in 1987, I took a new direction. I became the organizing pastor of a congregation of thirty-eight individuals. By the end of our second full year of operation we had an annual budget of $1 million, even though we still met in a rented building. By the end of 1990, our attendance had reached a thousand.

Two sets of four years, but between them some profound changes occurred in my life. At the mission organization I had worked hard—and done so by free choice. I gave myself to it completely, constantly seeking ways for the organization to grow and to expand the horizons of its outreach. Yet, when I looked deep into my own heart, I found myself asking, *Is my ministry becoming a higher priority than God?*

At first I felt guilty even asking the question. The organization had a unique vision to train Third World Christians and provided me with opportunities to teach and speak about Jesus Christ. Furthermore, I held a prestigious and privileged position. But I knew that work—even work for God—should not be taking first place in my life. I also knew that, whereas I was being very productive administratively, my position kept me away from the firsthand evangelism I felt God had called me to.

So I made my choice. It wasn't difficult. Once I knew that I wanted to be a pastor and teacher I began to seek an opportunity to serve God in a congregation. Over a period of three years, several pulpit committees interviewed me and, finally, right in Atlanta, where I had been living for nine years, came God's call to start a new church.

GOD'S CORPORATION: THE CALL OF A LIFETIME

I changed jobs. I left one organization (a parachurch ministry) and joined another (a church). But the important thing is this: I was able to make that switch because I distinguished two corporations. I don't mean the one I left and the one I joined; I mean the corporation that pays my wages and the corporation—God's corporation—to which I owe my highest loyalty.

Understanding our simultaneous membership in these two corporations is crucial. The fact that I may work for, say, the Ford Motor Company, doesn't give the Ford Motor Company or its personnel the right to demand anything they wish from me. In any conflict that arises between the demands of my work and the demands of my faith, it is my membership in *God's* corporation that takes priority. Because I am a Christian, I recognize that it is Jesus who occupies the executive suite.

> ## *Being a member of the two corporations creates unavoidable tension.*

In changing jobs, I responded to a directive from God's corporation. I did what God wanted me to do. It wasn't necessarily the smart move, either financially or in terms of prestige. Nor was it the move some of my closest friends would have wished me to make. But I knew that as an "employee" of God's corporation, I had to put God first.

I've met many Christian executives caught in the corporate rat race and also a good many Christian men and women below executive level who face similar challenges. Being a member of the two corporations creates unavoidable tension. Even if you work for a church-based organization, you will find yourself regularly asking questions such as the following:

How do I make decisions that are good for business and yet still morally right?
Is it possible to serve God *and* the corporation?
How do I do my job fully and yet not serve money?
Can I reconcile my personal needs and the needs of my family with the needs of my job?

What price am I being asked to pay for success?
What is most important in life, and how can I get it?

On virtually every level, Americans in the workforce are caught up in this dilemma of trying to meet the demands of their employment while keeping their integrity intact. Therefore, in this book I want to look at some of the things the Bible teaches Christians about work. It is not a how-to manual designed to give answers to every little problem a Christian might face. I want to look at a deeper level, at the main issues we need to get straight if we want to be conscientious Christians and productive workers.

God doesn't want you to be a bottom-line believer. He wants to transform your working life, just as He transforms your life at home and in your congregation. Jesus is the greatest leader who has ever lived. And He's your company Chairman.

1

PRIORITIES:

20/20 Vision

Ron's daughter Katie was born with a defective heart. The doctors predicted that she'd never survive to adulthood. She needed a lot of medical attention, a lot of love, a lot of stability.

Fortunately, because he lived in Atlanta, Ron had access to some of the top specialists in the field of cardiac medicine. He was also earning a good wage with a leading department store chain. But Ron had a problem. His work record was *so* outstanding that his company kept offering him promotions. A promotion meant more money, more prestige, another step up the career ladder. But it also meant relocating.

But mindful of Katie's needs, Ron turned down no less than *eight* promotion opportunities. The people "upstairs" in the executive suite couldn't figure it out. Why would a man turn down a fat salary increase and a wider variety of fringe benefits? Finally, they flew him to the corporate office for an interview.

Ron knew that the chips were down. If he rejected another offer, he could be terminated. So he told them the truth: "I love my work," he said, "and because I love it I work hard for the company. But you have to understand that my job comes third on my list of priorities."

"Third?" asked the astounded head of personnel. This was not what he'd expected to hear.

"God is first, and my family is next. If I don't have those two priorities right, I can't work. I won't put my job first."

Ron didn't get fired. But he didn't get a promotion either. Eventually his daughter died, just before her fifteenth birthday. Today he's still in his same job, with the same organization, unlikely ever to advance. But he has no regrets.

"I wouldn't sell my daughter's life for advancement in the company," he says. "I did what I believe is right."

Ron did not give his corporation blind allegiance. Nor did he allow his priorities to be dictated to him by short-term need. He knew exactly what was important in his life, and he knew in what order those things came. For Ron, only one person occupied the executive suite and called him to a lifetime commitment, and that person was Jesus.

RIGHT PRIORITIES

I believe that Ron's priorities were correct. In fact, they provide a model for all of us:

1. God
2. Family
3. Career

What does this mean for real life?

First, it means that nothing else takes God's place at the top. There are no takeovers in the divine corporation. Jesus stays in the executive suite forever: the job is for life. Anyone who puts family or career in front of God doesn't truly belong on the payroll.

Second, it means that career is important—but not as important as home. I know the CEO of one of the world's largest corporations. From the first day he went into business he dreamed of getting where he is today. And why not? Ambition is a God-given drive. But as Ron's example so clearly shows, God never asks us to sacrifice our family for the sake of our work. We should apply that rule flexibly, of course. Sometimes—especially if we're single—our family responsibilities may be looser. Also, in times of financial difficulty we may be forced to give less time to family than we'd like. But we should never lose sight of God's ideal: family, *then* work.

> ### *We need to keep our priorities in the right order and in right relation to each other.*

Third, prioritizing means that our own and our family's welfare are always secured by putting God first. During His earthly life, the Lord Jesus had a clearly defined vision. He knew from the start that He had come to do His Father's business. The time He spent in a carpenter's workshop did not distract Him, nor did the three years of seeing His disciples fumble and fail. Nothing deterred Him—not even the wishes of those He loved.

According to Scripture, "Jesus resolutely set out for Jerusalem" (Luke 9:51). He had set His face "like flint," as the book of Isaiah put it in a prophetic passage about the Messiah (Isaiah 50:7). He was going to Jerusalem no matter what went on around Him. He knew His destiny because He had a clear vision, a precisely set goal, a will to get through. Reaching major, top-priority goals takes effort; it costs. Sometimes it involves pleasing God rather than pleasing parents, spouse, or children.

In short, we need to keep our priorities in the right order *and* in right relation to each other. In the life of Jesus, God's call to Calvary came before anything His close friends or parents might have wished. It certainly came before His career as a carpenter. Yet He wasn't a workaholic. He wasn't so preoccupied with preaching that He never relaxed. He spent time socializing with the people who mattered most to Him—notably His disciples and friends, such as Lazarus, Martha, and Mary. The rush and bustle of His daily schedule didn't stop Him from staying up late at night to get away and talk to God. He was never too busy to talk to small children or to spend long periods of time with His inner circle of disciples.

The reason many people don't manage to get their priorities straight is that they don't defog their vision. It's as though they're walking around with misted eyeglasses. When I speak of vision, of course, I don't mean eyesight. Nor am I referring to dreams, fantasies, daydreams, delusions, or hallucinations. I don't even mean Paul's experience of being "caught up to the third heaven" (see 2 Corinthians 12:2). *Vision* in the sense I'm using it means "a sense of mission, a sense of being divinely called to accomplish a certain task." It is the ability to see needs and to make a commitment so single-minded that you will sweep aside every distraction in order to achieve the goal. In a way, "20/20 vision" is like tunnel vision—you see only your main task, and you don't divert energy into other things.

History is full of visionaries like this. Susannah Wesley, for example, vowed to bring up her children in the fear and nurture of the Lord. Had she departed from that task and failed to teach her sons in word and example, John and Charles Wesley would never have impacted the world as they did. More than two centuries later we still benefit from the principles they lived by and the vision their mother instilled in them.

But think also of Hudson Taylor's unswerving devotion to China, Amy Carmichael's lifelong commitment to India, and Jim Elliot's determination to "burn out" in service to Christ. Other visionaries were William Wilberforce, who persevered in his lifetime struggle to abolish the slave trade and outlaw slavery in all British dominions; David Livingstone and his obsession to open central Africa to Christian missions; and George Washington Carver, whose unrelenting drive to unlock the secrets of nature made him one of America's most remarkable individuals.

How, then, do we begin to develop a clear sense of vision? We need to look at four principles.

1. IF YOU WANT A VISION—DON'T GO LOOKING

A young man once came to my office and spent at least half an hour telling me of his lifelong desire "to be greatly used by God." I listened, struck by the fervency of his expression. Yet something kept bothering me. Finally I asked, "What are you doing now?"

"Waiting."

"For what?"

"For God to show me what to do."

"How long have you been waiting?"

"About a year," he said.

"*A year?* What have you been doing while you're waiting?"

He hesitated. Apparently he'd thought of little but his "spiritual anointing." He cleared his throat and said, "I've been waiting for holy guidance. I don't want to rush ahead of God."

"Are you working?"

"Well, ah, not really," he said. "Mostly, I've been praying and reading the Bible—you know, waiting."

"How do you support yourself?"

"Oh, my parents."

"How old are you?"

"Twenty-nine."

"You mean," I asked, "that you're nearly thirty, and you still make your parents pay all your bills and take care of you?"

"I don't make them do that," he said. "I let them. They love me." He looked blank. Clearly he didn't understand why I would bother to question this. He said, "You see, I'm preparing myself to do a special work for God—"

"And what about responsibility?"

"Oh, I'm ready to do anything God asks."

"No, I mean your responsibility now. What about God's commandment, 'Honor your father and your mother'?" This time he was so shocked he just looked at me.

I said, "You're willing to let them work hard to take care of you, but you're doing nothing for them in return." Yet he wore expensive clothing. He was neatly groomed, even down to his manicured nails. Only afterward did it strike me that I should have told him about Stephen and Philip.

Early in the life of the church, when the believers tried to live and work together communally, a conflict arose. The Greek-speaking Jewish widows complained that they weren't getting an equal share of the food. Peter knew that the food distribution was important and needed to be handled with integrity. But he also knew that the apostles had more pressing work than acting as table waiters. So he asked the believers themselves to select seven men of high spiritual caliber to look after the logistics of food distribution.

These were spiritual men: according to Acts 6:3 they were of good standing, "full of the Spirit and wisdom." Yet they did not see themselves as being above a humble, practical task. They didn't sit around waiting for some grander opportunity to present itself. They did what they knew had to be done, working at a humble job until the day came when God enlarged their ministries. Their waiting was active and responsible.

The book of Acts tells us what happened to two of the seven. Stephen, "a man full of God's grace and power, did great wonders and miraculous signs among the people" (Acts 6:8) and witnessed so fearlessly for Jesus Christ that he became the church's first martyr. Philip is later called an evangelist, and the memorable story of his preaching to a treasury official of the Ethiopian queen Candace is recorded in Acts 8:26–39.

Both men earned their ministries. They were chosen because they had already shown they could be trusted. What their personal ambitions were we will never know. We do know that they waited patiently for God to unfold His plan for them and that while they waited they made themselves useful.

Getting a vision from God is a little like staying upright on a bicycle.

In contrast to Stephen and Philip, the young man who wanted to do "a great work for God" may appear an extreme case. But he's not. There are plenty of Christians who wait passively for a mission to overtake them, meanwhile doing nothing to build their characters or prove their reliability or commitment. They're ready for action, they say, as soon as God speaks. But they're not sure what they want to do. They don't volunteer, they don't even say yes when asked. They think God will one day show them a bright light in the sky, call their names, and appoint them a major task. But until that moment, how do they live? What do they do? Who feeds them?

This outlook is almost incomprehensible to those of us who have immigrated to the United States from other countries and who see America as a land of infinite possibility. We were taught that hard work and perseverance were all it took. We learned that a man born in a log cabin could become president of the United States, that a fruit picker could become a multimillionaire. At the very least, in America a person is expected to *get on with it*. And that, I believe, is exactly what God expects us to do.

In this respect, getting a vision from God is a little like staying upright on a bicycle: it's a great deal easier if you're already moving. As I read through the Bible, I don't find a single instance of a man or woman being pushed into service from a state of *idleness*. The vision and the mission arise through the things they're already doing.

The story of David makes the point clearly. As the youngest in the family—the one left behind to tend the sheep while his big brothers went to war—David seemed least likely to attain military honors or become Israel's warrior-king. He arrived at the battlefront not to join active service but to deliver food. Only when he got there and began to pick up the camp gossip did he realize that his experience as a shepherd had prepared him for an entirely new calling. However much his peers derided him, David was no pushover. It was by defending the herds on the mountainsides of Israel that he'd perfected his skill with the slingshot—the only weapon with which the Philistine giant Goliath could be slain. No one in the army could teach David that. Had he joined the army with his brothers at the beginning of the war, he'd have been just another big-talking foot soldier.

The examples are many. Esther had no idea when she married King Xerxes that God would use her to save the Jews in Persia. Amos had planned a career in fruit picking before God called him to prophesy. All these individuals engaged wholeheartedly in their normal occupations and concerns, quietly proving their faithfulness, unaware of the vision that God would break upon them.

To be sure, their ordinary lives often called for courage and moral strength. Look at Joseph. Anyone who's read Joseph's story in Genesis will remember how his gift for interpreting dreams landed him the most important job in Egypt. But where did this calling come to him? In prison: the rumor of Joseph's unusual powers reached the troubled Pharaoh through a servant who'd once been Joseph's cell mate. And why was Joseph in prison? Because he had refused to become a toy-boy for Potiphar's wife. In other words, proving his moral worth—and taking the consequences—set up precisely that train of events by which God's greater vision was revealed.

A similar pattern occurred a few generations later in the life of Moses:

> *By faith Moses, when he had grown up, refused to be known as the son of Pharaoh's daughter. He chose to be mistreated along with the people of God rather than to enjoy the pleasures of sin for a short time. He regarded disgrace for the sake of Christ as of greater value than the treasures of Egypt, because he was looking ahead to his reward. By faith he left Egypt, not fearing the king's anger; he persevered because he saw him who is invisible. (Hebrews 11:24–27)*

Moses' weakness lay not so much in overeagerness for a calling as in his reluctance to accept it when it came. The faith in which he led the people out of Egypt was punctuated by a good many bouts of self-doubt and threats to resign. Nevertheless, like Joseph, Moses had deliberately taken the harder route. So much did he live by his loyalty to God's people that he killed one of the Egyptian oppressors, an act for which he suffered a lengthy exile. Yet, had he not been exiled, he would not have ended up tending sheep for Jethro. Nor, one day, would he have seen the burning bush.

2. VISION LEADS TO SERVICE

The story of the burning bush requires some study. At first God seems to be talking only about Himself:

> *The Lord said, "I have indeed seen the misery of my people in Egypt. I have heard them crying out because of their slave drivers, and I am concerned about their suffering. So I have come down to rescue them from the hand of the Egyptians and to bring them up out of that land into a good and spacious land, a land flowing with milk and honey." (Exodus 3:7–8)*

Hearing this, Moses might well have replied, "Terrific! When are you going to begin?" But there was a sting in the tail, and that sting was the vision: "So now, go. I am sending you to Pharaoh to bring my people the Israelites out of Egypt" (verse 10).

Unlike the young man who came to visit me, Moses had never actively sought a vision from God. He snooped around the burning bush out of simple curiosity. Confronted now with a divine mission, he began to retreat as fast as he could: "Who am I, that I should go to Pharaoh and bring the Israelites out of Egypt?" (verse 11).

But there was no escape. The vision had come, and the vision, like all divine visions, was one of *service* to others. True, in the course of fulfilling that vision Moses became the most influential figure in Jewish history. He was given amazing supernatural powers—the ability to turn a staff into a snake and to chop a sea in half. He faced down the man every Egyptian feared: Pharaoh. Yet he sought none of these things.

I'm not saying that Moses had a carefree life—nobody who is without worries would call his son *Gershom* (which means "I have become an alien in a foreign land" [Exodus 2:22]). But, no doubt, on the day he saw the burning bush

Moses had woken up as usual, content to be a family man—healthy, settled, and with a safe job. Leading the Israelites out of Egypt would have seemed to him an absurd flight of fancy. In two respects, then, Moses' life is a pattern for our own.

First, Moses didn't sit in the scrub fantasizing about the day he'd return to Egypt and settle the score. He didn't want power. Hunger for power has never been a worthy goal in God's terms. When Jesus' disciples saw their work in power terms, they received a sharp rap on the knuckles:

> *[Jesus] sent messengers on ahead, who went into a Samaritan village to get things ready for him; but the people there did not welcome him, because he was heading for Jerusalem. When the disciples James and John saw this, they asked, "Lord, do you want us to call fire down from heaven to destroy them?" But Jesus turned and rebuked them. (Luke 9:52–55)*

The young man who came to see me wanted "a powerful ministry"—that's exactly how he put it. And that's one explanation for his inactivity. He saw value only in power, and, because the kind of power he dreamed of comes only from God, he just sat on his hands waiting for God to empower him.

But, second, it makes far more sense to prepare yourself when you know what you're preparing for. The waiting, the analysis, the self-examination—these things come *after* the vision, not before. Having seen the burning bush, Moses spent months consulting with Jethro, undertaking the long journey back to Egypt, and then meeting with Aaron and the Israelite elders. Plenty of time for reflection there.

"It seems to me," I told the young man before he left, "that you have the sequence wrong. Jesus commissioned His disciples to go into all the world. So they had a vision, a mandate to preach and teach. Once they had the calling, they then waited and prayed."

3. DON'T BUILD EMPIRES

It is not enough to have a *sense* of mission or to *feel* the call to serve. Nor is it enough to talk about the mission as though we were already engaged in it. Along with the call comes the responsibility to act. Paul felt this so keenly that he cried out, "When I preach the gospel, I cannot boast, for I am compelled to preach. Woe to me if I do not preach the gospel!" (1 Corinthians 9:16).

Acting on a mission, though, brings its own temptations. People who talk loudly about "God's vision" and "God's plan" may, deep down, be serving their egos. They see to it that institutions get named after them. They lap up attention and praise as though these were their due. I've actually heard Christians say of the rewards of service, "I worked hard for this." They really think they deserve recognition.

This contrasts sharply with Jesus' attitude. I have yet to find any statement in the Gospels saying that His name was chiseled into a temple cornerstone or that a university chair was named after Him. If he sought a legacy at all, it was the legacy of *people*. Thirty years after His death there existed no Jesus Memorial Hospital. But hundreds, thousands, of people recalled meeting Jesus and carried in their minds the searing imprint of His personality and teaching. Jesus could have used His position to gain power, popularity, and pleasure. He was tempted by the Devil to do exactly that— to achieve His goals *without* undergoing the painful trial of crucifixion. But He chose the harder path.

Likewise with Paul. When the Corinthians finally goaded Paul into presenting his credentials, the list made strange reading. No global mission organization with Paul's name on the letterhead. No staggering statistics of conversions achieved. No awe-inspiring names on a board of trustees. Instead, comparing himself to more charismatic church leaders, Paul asks,

Are they servants of Christ? (I am out of my mind to talk like this.) I am more. I have worked much harder, been in prison more fre-

quently, been flogged more severely, and been exposed to death again and again. Five times I received from the Jews the forty lashes minus one. Three times I was beaten with rods, once I was stoned, three times I was shipwrecked. (2 Corinthians 11:23–25)

Jesus and Paul fulfilled their visions and passed the visions on to others. By contrast, the vision of empire builders follows them to the grave. In the secular world, contrast the achievements of philanthropists Andrew Carnegie, J. C. Penney, and John Wanamaker with those of Ivan Boesky and Michael Miliken, two men who made billions through illegal currency trading; or Charles Keating, infamous for the savings-and-loans scandal. These men— like Carnegie, Penney, and Wanamaker—could have served the nation's needs, ensured safe retirement through financial investments, lifted heavy burdens from the shoulders of the poor. Instead, they chose personal success; they had no vision of what they could do for the world.

Skill alone, then, is nothing. It builds egos and nothing more. But marry skill to a godly vision—that is, acknowledge the source of your skill and put it to proper use—and you will see marvels.

I remember meeting a woman from Michigan named Linda. She was a new convert to the faith and extraordinarily gifted. Already highly successful as an interior decorator, she'd realized she could also write about her faith. She wrote so well and so naturally that her articles never got rejected. I said to Linda, "You obviously have a gift. And along with that gift has come an awesome responsibility."

That responsibility, which bears on all of us, is to be like the boy Samuel. When God called in the dead of night, Eli taught Samuel to answer, "Speak, for your servant is listening" (1 Samuel 3:10). Samuel listened to God, and when he grew up, we are told, "Samuel's word came to all Israel" (4:1). The listening remains central to all visions. You don't get the vision and then take it away like so much capital and invest it for your own ends. Repeatedly you bring it back to God. That's why I ask myself, with every decision and every plan, "Do I want to glorify God, or do I want to leave a legacy of my powerful ego?" Again and again the Lord Jesus tells us how He sought to glorify the Father, to honor the Father, and to obey the Father. We should do likewise.

4. SMALL VISIONS ARE AS GOOD AS BIG ONES

I sometimes reflect on the young man who came to see me and wonder what lay behind his obsession with doing a "great work for God." One factor, I'm sure, had to do with expectations. Most of the biblical individuals I've mentioned in this chapter are monumental figures, people numbered among the great and the good, people whose passion and commitment act as an incentive to our own: Moses, Paul, David, and, supremely, Jesus Himself. But not everyone in God's corporation is called to a vision of this scale. God's purposes rely, in the main, on ordinary people grasping visions that are a good bit less dramatic than Moses' or Paul's—less dramatic, but no less important.

Jesus' parable of the talents makes a close link between divine calling and our ability to do the job. The man setting out on his journey, Jesus says, gave to "each according to his ability" (Matthew 25:15). At first this might imply that the church is a kind of "meritocracy": an organization where the most talented people get the highest rewards. But nowhere is this implied in the parable. Jesus does not say that the man who received five talents was smarter than the man who received two. Rather, both were given a mission—a vision—that pushed them to the limits of their potential, and, accordingly, both were rewarded in the same way: "You have been faithful with a few things; I will put you in charge of many things" (Matthew 25:21, 23). If one man received two talents and not five, it was to prevent him from being overloaded. That is why the man who got one talent—and buried it—was treated with as much severity as if he'd gotten five.

What matters is to be faithful in the vision we have. It's only by seeing the importance of the apparently ordinary and mundane that we can let our vision expand. The people who grow and mature are the ones who keep stepping forward, using their God-given insight and ability. God gives us the chance to prove ourselves, and, as we progress, so our vision enlarges. "Whoever can be trusted with very little can also be trusted with much" (Luke 16:10). That's the corporate policy when Jesus, the Chairman of the board, calls us to a lifetime of service—and what CEO would deny that it makes sense?

2

INTEGRITY:
You're One Person, Not Two

A mogul brought his corporation out of a protract-
ed slump in just three years. While waiting for
him to emerge from the annual stockholders' meeting, a
national reporter referred to this CEO as "a devoted husband and family man, and an active churchgoer." The network showed clips of the man and his wife giving food to
hungry families in a region of the country devastated by
floods and tornadoes. Another clip showed him with a
crowd of worshipers in a church service.

When he came out of the stockholders' meeting, he was
smiling. Why not? He had just received a bonus in excess of
$100,000. And he knew his job. As he said to the reporter,
"The top line in business is profit. The bottom line in business is profit."

But as the reporter followed him outside, the camera
panned a crowd of picketers. They carried signs calling the
corporation unfair and unfeeling. Several of the signs said
harsh things about the CEO as well. These men and women
had been laid off at plants across the country. One man
yelled out, "How about a bonus for us?" Others jeered at the
CEO, holding up placards demanding that the company
consider their needs.

The CEO ignored the crowd—perhaps for his own safety—and got into a chauffeur-driven limousine. Without
commenting on the pickets, the reporter made some inane

remark about the industriousness of the big man. Immediately the station segued into a commercial.

At that point I turned off the television. I sat quietly and thought about the scene I had watched. Was the mogul an uncaring man? He had obviously done an outstanding job for his organization, otherwise the stockholders wouldn't have voted him such a large bonus. What about the hundred or so people outside the building? The crowd apparently represented more than 20,000 employees who had been let go. Did the CEO know any of them personally? Did he struggle with his conscience over the layoffs, assessing his policies from an *ethical* standpoint, not just in terms of profit-making? Did he have any idea of the difficulties faced by the laid-off workers? Did he care?

I've never met this talented man, and at that distance I may be misjudging him. On the other hand, nothing I saw on the TV clip, nor anything I've heard about him since, suggests that he had compassion for the people who were once his employees. Yet he was known in the community as an individual who cared about others. Could he really be both hard-hearted and compassionate at the same time?

This is an unkind comparison, but the CEO reminded me of the godfather in the films of the same name. In one of the movies, the don is shown holding an audience with those who need his help. One man begs for an operation to save the life of his child. The don listens carefully, then gives instructions that the money be provided. The man kisses his hand. On that evidence alone you'd judge the don to be a man of compassion, even a soft touch. Yet in the very next scene this same don dispatches two hit men to commit a murder. The assassination is shown in all its gory detail. After that the don comes home for dinner. He sits down at a large, oval table with his wife and children and grandchildren, all of them laughing, chatting, and enjoying themselves.

Now, the average CEO doesn't go around rewarding disloyalty with extermination. But the personality split occurring in the fictional don's mind occurs in much the same way in the minds of many legitimately wealthy men. Somehow compassion and callousness seem able to live side by side within one individual. You'd almost say that such people had two distinct personalities—one they presented to their immediate family and loyal supporters, and another they reserved for their enemies and those who stood in the way of their ambition.

We give thanks that *we're* not like that. Or are we . . . ?

SCHIZO-CHRISTIANS

A few years ago a friend introduced me to a well-known and successful East Coast businessman. I'll call him Ben. He was a prominent church leader who contributed heavily to God's work. In fact, I'd heard about him because he'd given generously to famine relief in Ethiopia a few years earlier. Several people had said that Ben was "a man who cares."

The three of us had lunch together so that Ben could hear more about the missionary project to which I hoped he might make a donation. Ben was on a high. He told us he'd just completed one of his best business deals. Our mutual friend pushed him to give us the details. But as he did so it became increasingly obvious that, whereas not illegal in a technical sense, Ben's conduct in securing the deal was, to say the least, morally questionable.

Finally my friend smiled and said, "I'm now talking to Ben the businessman, aren't I?" Ben laughed.

My friend turned to me and said, "Ben is two people. Sometimes he's Ben the Christian, and sometimes he's Ben the money-making entrepreneur. Whenever we get together, I have to stay on guard until I find out which I'm talking to."

Both men laughed at the remark. Evidently flattered, Ben said, "He has me pretty well figured out, doesn't he?"

He wasn't ashamed. He didn't apologize. In fact, the man reveled in his hypocrisy. The laughter was embarrassing.

A few minutes later, the conversation switched tracks as Ben started talking about his involvement in Ethiopia. Tears filled his eyes, and his voice grew husky. It astonished me to see the abrupt change. I chided myself for being judgmental about him, concluding that I hadn't properly understood the story of his business venture. Yet the meeting left a bad taste. I said little during our time together.

What was wrong with Ben? Couldn't he see that his business practices were inconsistent with ethical behavior? For a non-Christian to be inconsistent is at least understandable. But in God's corporation, where Jesus is Chairman of the board, why do we find such a glaring example of hypocrisy?

THE DEVIL IN MIDDLE MANAGEMENT?

As I returned from the meeting with Ben, Jesus' words from the Sermon on the Mount kept coming to me. When I got home, I looked them up:

> *Watch out for false prophets. They come to you in sheep's clothing, but inwardly they are ferocious wolves. By their fruit you will recognize them. Do people pick grapes from thornbushes, or figs from thistles? Likewise every good tree bears good fruit, but a bad tree bears bad fruit. A good tree cannot bear bad fruit, and a bad tree cannot bear good fruit. Every tree that does not bear good fruit is cut down and thrown into the fire. Thus, by their fruit you will recognize them. (Matthew 7:15–20)*

It would have been easy to categorize Ben as a bad tree bearing bad fruit. But the analysis didn't quite fit. Clearly Ben wasn't a false prophet in the way Jesus meant. In at least two major areas of his life—his family and his philanthropy—he seemed to have a truly Christian spirit. Besides, I hesitated (rightly) to issue that kind of judgment on Ben. Having met him only once, who was I to say whether Ben was a Christian or not? Only God knows that.

Sin regularly breaks out in our lives through careless words and thoughtless actions and urges to put our own interests first.

Next, I mulled over the psychological angles. Maybe there was something about Ben's makeup that prevented him from letting go of the aggressive all-or-nothing behavior patterns that dominated his business life. This certainly had made sense in other cases I have known. There's the high-rolling bank executive named Roland, who teaches an adult Sunday school class. Maybe I should call him an exhorter, because he pleads with his fellow Christians to live their lives for Jesus Christ. Sometimes tears come to his eyes as he urges them to be more committed. Yet at home Roland verbally abuses his four sons. They get lengthy and loud lectures about how they don't measure up and how they need to improve. One son has already experimented with drugs. Roland's difficulty may well have its roots in psychology. His passionate pleas—to his class and to his children—suggest he's less than satisfied with his own behavior. He sets impossibly high standards for others because he himself feels inadequate.

Be that as it may, in the end I think there is a deeper and simpler explanation for the kind of split personality exhibited by people like Ben and Roland. After all, they are not unique. They show in two extreme forms the kind of inconsistency to which every Christian is prone, including you and me. We're all a mixture. We're all a strange concoction of motives and actions, a muddle of good and bad, Christlikeness and sin. Any Christian who claims to have licked sin this side of eternity is simply deluded.

Underlying our new nature as Christians is an old, sinful nature that will remain active in us until the day we die. Our salvation condemns it but does not immediately remove it. And the result is that all of us, to one degree or another, are inconsistent. At any moment we can slip back into the old patterns of behavior. It happens all the time. Sin regularly breaks out in our lives through careless words and thoughtless actions and urges to put our own interests first.

It happens when we least expect it. As a minister, I know that one of the most vulnerable times for most Christians is after they've received a blessing. It's upon leaving the church on a high, walking on spiritual air, that Christian couples are apt to have their biggest fights. Or they come into church, looking forward to fellowship and meeting God in a special way, and somebody pulls into their parking spot. What unprintable language comes out of the mouths that in a few minutes will be praising God!

I'm not being patronizing here. When I get in my car, I always *mean* to be courteous and kind, yet I don't always drive that way. And I'm sure that if the apostle Paul had lived in the age of the automobile, he'd have said the same thing. Read Romans and you'll find him going through the theology of sin step by step: from the first Adam's fall to the Second Adam's redemption of humanity through the cross. If we live in Jesus, Paul said, sin has no claim on us. Yet, as he admitted in Romans 7, the habit of sin is incredibly hard to shake off:

> *We know that the law is spiritual; but I am unspiritual, sold as a slave to sin. I do not understand what I do. For what I want to do I do not do, but what I hate I do. And if I do what I do not want to do, I agree that the law is good. As it is, it is no longer I myself who do it, but it is sin living in me. I know that nothing good lives in me, that is, in my sinful nature. For I have the desire to do what is good, but I cannot carry it out. For what I do is not the good I want to do; no, the evil I do not want to do—this I keep on doing. Now if I do what I do not want to do, it is no longer I who do it, but it is sin living in me that does it. . . . What a wretched man I am! Who will rescue me from this body of death? Thanks be to God—through Jesus Christ our Lord! (verses 14–20, 24–25)*

I used to hear preachers quote this passage and say it was Paul's picture of life *before* meeting Jesus Christ. They insisted that when Paul wrote "Thanks be to God" he meant us to understand that he was *already* rescued from "this body of death"—that the struggle had ended and that as a Christian he lived in a state of constant victory. The longer I'm a believer, however, the more convinced I become that this passage has to do with Paul's life *after* he came to Christ. He was saying, "I know what's right. I just can't do the right thing on my own"—so much so that sometimes he barely understood his own actions.

That makes a lot of sense to me. Sin is pervasive. We are capable of wrongdoing at every moment of our lives. We sometimes act from the wrong motives without even knowing what those motives are. And we have a marvelous capacity for self-delusion. In other words, we can be shocked when we see in others the sins we are—in our weakness—just as capable of committing ourselves.

STONES AND GLASS HOUSES

A Christian I know named Pete told me about a company staff meeting he attended. It was a long session, made necessary by a string of company failures, and Pete's supervisor—also a Christian but more experienced than Pete—was getting blamed for a lot of things that really weren't his fault. Finally, the supervisor snapped—and swore. A few minutes later they broke for coffee.

Pete, still shaken, was sipping his coffee when his boss walked over. Pete confronted him. "You're the one who taught me about God. But you shocked me today. You're a Christian. I never expected you—of all people—to use such language."

"I was wrong," his supervisor admitted. "I guess it shows I'm human."

Pete walked away, shaking his head. One outburst, perhaps, he could have handled. But in the following days the scene was repeated again and again, and in the end Pete decided to ask for a transfer. Before he did so, he went to his pastor. "How can I continue to work under a man like that?" he asked.

For a few minutes they talked about sin and imperfections in others and in ourselves. Intellectually Pete understood his pastor's words. But, although he had been a Christian for nearly two years, it was the first flagrant inconsistency he'd witnessed.

"Pete," the pastor said, "when you became a Christian, God forgave you. Right?"

"Definitely."

"Will you ever need to be forgiven again?"

"Sure. I mean, I fail all the time."

Normally the pastor would have pushed ahead, but this time he felt restrained and instead allowed Pete's own words to bounce back at him. After a long silence Pete mumbled, "Oh. He was only being true to his sinful nature, wasn't he?"

Suddenly he didn't need to explain away his boss's lapse. But neither did he need to overlook it. He understood the practical implication of sin in the human heart. Just like Paul, his boss struggled with sin, even though he was redeemed in Christ. Pete knew that struggle by personal experience. He should, I think, have been quicker to recognize it in someone else.

This kind of doublethink is common in the church. When we fail, most of us suffer guilt, ask God to forgive, and then continue our pilgrimage, knowing we'll fail again. Yet when others fail—especially leaders—we're shocked, angry, and often vindictive.

Witness, for instance, the scandal over Jim Bakker and the PTL television network. I didn't watch their programs; I never sent them money; almost everything they did I disagreed with. But when Jim Bakker came to court, I was frankly ashamed of the attitude of many of my Christian brothers and sisters. I expected finger-pointing and condemnation from people *outside* the church; but from those in Christ I naively expected compassion and understanding. But I found nothing in the torrent of media abuse to tell me whether it came from believers or nonbelievers.

I want to be clear that I oppose wrongdoing, and I believe that Jim Bakker and the others involved are answerable for what they did. Justice is as much a characteristic of our God as is compassion. But the Christians who commented on the scandal were so eager in their denunciations that they appeared to have almost no grasp either of the *universality* of sin or of its immense capacity to deceive.

DON'T BE DUPED!

Look at the story of sin's origin in the Bible. Note that in Genesis 3, when Satan spoke to Eve, he didn't appeal to base instincts for power or pleasure. Instead, he convinced her that she would actually be doing *good* by disobeying God. She would be able to make moral decisions, she would be wise, she would be like God Himself:

> *"You will not surely die," the serpent said to the woman. "For God knows that when you eat of it your eyes will be opened, and you will be like God, knowing good and evil."*
>
> *When the woman saw that the fruit of the tree was good for food and pleasing to the eye, and also desirable for gaining wisdom, she took some and ate it. She also gave some to her husband, who was with her, and he ate it. Then the eyes of both of them were opened, and they realized they were naked. (verses 4–7)*

Sin doesn't like to show its true nature. Instead, it disguises itself—in hundreds of ways. For instance, we can deliberately hurt someone's feelings and yet justify our behavior by calling it "honest" or "truthful." Just like the serpent, we pass off something bad as something good. Sin lures us into all kinds of wrong behavior—meanness, ingratitude, dishonesty, revenge—by persuading us first that the action is consistent with God's law. Christians are peculiarly susceptible to this. I'm fairly sure that, at the time they sin, many Christians sincerely believe they're being helpful, perhaps even kind. Satan has only to convince us that we're doing the right thing for the right motives, and we're hooked.

This in no way mitigates the wrongdoing—sin remains sin. But it should help us understand how Christians can get drawn into sinning. It should also encourage us to exercise a little compassion toward those who fall, but it should also put us on our guard. The deceitfulness of sin is easy to see when it comes to young people and spouses.

Show me a rebellious adolescent and I will show you a child convinced by Satan that his parents don't love him.

Once Satan succeeds in convincing teenagers of this lie, they feel justified in drinking and taking drugs and experimenting with illicit sex. Their parents' insensitivity (as they see it) relieves them of responsibility for their actions. Sometimes they even see it as demanding a kind of revenge. Talk to some teenagers about the hurt their parents feel, and the response is, "They deserve it. After all, they don't love me."

In the same way, an unfaithful husband will often say, "My wife never loved me. She never showed me compassion or understanding." Here, again, Satan succeeds in persuading a Christian that sinning is necessary to achieve justice. Feeling that he *deserves* to be the object of lavish love and tenderness, the husband sees himself as the victim of his wife's insensitivity. No attention is paid to his own role in drying up the relationship. As he sees it, justice almost *demands* that he be unfaithful. "She deserved the hurt she got because she has been such an unloving person."

This is satanic deception! And in case you think you're immune to it, let me remind you of the ringing words of George Whitefield: "But for the grace of God, there go I." I believe that, except for God's grace, I could just as easily do some of the sinful things others do. Perhaps I am just as guilty, but my own sinfulness doesn't allow me to see it!

> *When accused, the natural human tendency is to wriggle out of it and blame somebody else.*

During the height of the Jim Bakker trial, a friend said, "Michael, don't you realize why people are so harsh about the PTL scandal?" Without waiting for an answer, he said, "Because it hits close to home. It's too strong a reminder of their own sinful nature." Then he laughed. "See, I got caught up in it too. I said *their* sinful nature, not *ours*."

As we continued our conversation, he said, "You know, it's the old business of pointing the finger at someone else to keep the focus off yourself." Immediately I thought of

Genesis again. That's exactly how the first humans behaved when confronted with their sin:

> And [God] said, "Who told you that you were naked? Have you eaten from the tree that I commanded you not to eat from?"
> The man said, "The woman you put here with me—she gave me some fruit from the tree, and I ate it."
> Then the Lord God said to the woman, "What is this you have done?"
> The woman said, "The serpent deceived me, and I ate."
> (3:11–13)

When we are accused, the natural human tendency is to wriggle out of it and blame somebody else. But we can't fool God. After the Fall, He confronted both the woman and the man, giving them no chance to deny their disobedience. And—I'm glad to say—He's just as careful with us.

LOOK AT YOURSELF—AND KEEP LOOKING

Acknowledging that Jesus is in the executive suite doesn't mean that no one in the organization fails. Everybody fails, time after time. The way forward is not to deny it, or to pretend that the failure is incidental, but to confront it daily. Leaders, particularly, will never deal adequately with the question of sin in counseling and guiding others until they admit the sin in themselves. Until they can say—and mean— "Wretched soul that I am, who will save me?" they don't know what sin is about.

God calls us to examine ourselves regularly. We should not treat sin lightly. We should be alert to it, recognize it, plan against it, review our strategies for evading it. And we should not do any of these things outside our relationship to the Boss. There is, after all, a company policy on sin. Here is a good strategy.

1. Talk about sin in the present tense. Remember that, although God forgives our sins, the sinful nature isn't something from which God delivers us once and for all. Sin moves right along with us until we reach the grave. To live is to be tempted, and without the grace of God at work in us and without the sustaining power of the Holy Spirit, we'll fall.

2. Focus on the small sins. The "big" sins—such as murder, theft, adultery—may look dangerous, but they depend on combinations of motive and opportunity that are comparatively rare. For most of us, it's the little sins that cause the problem, not just because the temptations arise more frequently but because sin, like cancer, will spread if it isn't checked. Consequently, the so-called little sins (an angry retort, an impure motive, a thoughtless action) need as much, if not more, attention than the big ones. It's no coincidence that the Bible concentrates on verbal sins: gossiping, backbiting, murmuring, criticizing. These temptations face us every day. We have motives and opportunities in plenty.

3. Avoid affirmations. It is no help to tackle sin with self-congratulatory affirmations such as "I am great." That is actually only another part of Satan's deception. Affirmations are helpful, but only *after* identifying and dealing with sin. The reason is that affirmations alone don't change anything. It's like when my son is told to tidy his room. He pushes everything under the bed and then tells his mother, "Come and look. Everything's clean!"

4. Keep everything you do under review. The world is full of Christians who pay attention to sin on Sunday morning, but on Monday morning they seem to enter some alternative universe where sin isn't an issue. What people do on Monday in the boardroom or the kitchen is every bit as important to God as what they do on Sunday at church. By the same token, Christian parents should ensure that the advice they give their children when other adult Christians are around is the same they give in private. And drivers (myself included) should drive with just as much care on their own as they do when passengers are in the car.

5. Don't close your eyes and hope sin will go away. It won't. After they'd sampled the forbidden fruit, Adam and Eve tried to pretend nothing had happened:

Then the eyes of both of them were opened, and they realized they were naked; so they sewed fig leaves together and made coverings for themselves. . . . But the Lord God called to the man, "Where are you?"

He answered, "I heard you in the garden, and I was afraid because I was naked; so I hid."

And he said, "Who told you that you were naked? Have you eaten from the tree that I commanded you not to eat from?" (Genesis 3:7, 9–11)

Right from the beginning, sin has labored to cover itself up. Adam and Eve didn't become naked as a result of sinning: they were naked already. But sin gave their nakedness a symbolic edge. They were exposed, literally and symbolically, and they didn't like it. That inner nakedness—that guilt—has remained with the human race ever since, and we have never tired in our efforts at covering it up. We'll never succeed. We can call sin something else, or put a more favorable gloss on our motives, but at the end of the day, sin is still sin.

Being in God's corporation, the church, ought to help. After all, sin is everyone's problem—just as security is everyone's problem in a downtown office building. And if we are truly members of the same spiritual body, we should have an interest in helping one another to overcome it. How tragic that in many cases Christians feel themselves to be in competition with one another and that the struggle to beat sin becomes instead a mechanism by which sin—in the form of pride and one-upmanship—tightens its hold.

3

SUCCESS:
Be Unbending Where It Matters

I really admire that man," said one of my lunch companions when the name of a multimillionaire came up. "He's the most successful man I know."

"And he started out as a poor boy with a ne'er-do-well father," said the other. "I wonder what drove him—what made him such a success."

It's a common question. In a society that places such a premium on individual achievement, anyone who reaches the top of his or her field, who makes a fortune or achieves celebrity status, is inevitably asked, "What's the secret of your success?" We want to know what makes this person different from the rest of us. We think that if we found out we might be able to succeed as well.

People answer the question in a thousand ways when interviewed by the media. The high achievers will list one, two, three, maybe ten qualities that set them apart. Usually they cite factors such as hard work and commitment. Once I heard one say, "Just lucky." That may be closer to the truth. For every hardworking and committed achiever, you'll find a dozen men and women who've made the same effort but haven't come anything close to the same scale. On the face of it, much seems to rely on happenstance, luck, the roll of the dice—not least because of the sheer number of factors involved and the difficulty of isolating any single influence.

That seems to be the case, for instance, when we look at a church's "success" in achieving congregational growth. Not surprisingly, the question of what drives growth has been the subject of much analysis since the church growth movement began in the late 1970s. Christian magazines have featured fast-growing churches; dozens of books have rolled off the press. Pastors, evangelists, and social scientists have each pronounced on what he or she sees as the critical factor—and almost none of them has said the same thing.

One pastor in southern California claimed that his church grew because of his positive preaching and his emphasis on the "priesthood of believers." No doubt both of them helped to swell his attendance figures. But at another church in the very same community, equally big and growing equally fast, the emphasis was placed less on theology and more on people-related activities and social outreach. Several occult-based religious groups have also sprung up and flourished in that same city.

Ultimately, the reasons for growth remain obscure even to the ministers who preside over it. As one pastor commented, "When God is ready to produce fruit in any location, it seems that no matter what church or group goes to work, they prosper." From one perspective, it looks like we're back to luck.

THE CALL TO BE OUT IN FRONT

As Christians, of course, we don't believe in luck. God works in accordance with His divine purpose, even though the nature of that purpose often remains hidden. That doesn't mean we regard His purpose as inscrutable; unlike Muslims, we do not accept either fortune or misfortune passively as the "will of Allah." But we are required to live in awareness of, and submission to, a "corporate plan" whose wider dimensions we may not comprehend. This idea can be seen in many scriptures:

Give thanks in all circumstances, for this is God's will for you in Christ Jesus. (1 Thessalonians 5:18)

No temptation has seized you except what is common to man. And God is faithful; he will not let you be tempted beyond what you can bear. But when you are tempted, he will also provide a way out so that you can stand up under it. (1 Corinthians 10:13)

And we know that in all things God works for the good of those who love him, who have been called according to his purpose . . . to be conformed to the likeness of his Son, that he might be the firstborn among many brothers. (Romans 8:28–29)

This puts all Christians on a par. Further, we're all human, we're all sinners, we're all mortal. "There is no difference," wrote Paul in Romans 3:22–24, "for all have sinned and fall short of the glory of God, and are justified freely by his grace through the redemption that came by Christ Jesus." Every one of us receives this inheritance, and, on the basis of it, every one of us is exhorted to follow after righteousness, to strive to be our best, to reach forward.

Having said that, however, God's corporation seems, from its foundation, to have taken on much the same thinking about achievement as can be found in secular society. Some men and women have stood a little taller than those around them. The apostle Paul is a good example. He was the central figure of the early church. Even today we refer to him as the greatest writer of the New Testament, the chief apostle, the most outstanding Christian of the first century. And much the same is true of our own generation. Asked to name a "great Christian," most people will cite a celebrity— a leading evangelist, or someone like Mother Teresa, whose life is thought to exemplify humble service to others.

As I said earlier, there's a danger here. Hold up any individual as a paragon of Christian virtue, and you are likely to end up with factions. That's exactly what happened in the Corinthian church, and it drew Paul's sternest rebuke:

For when one says, "I follow Paul," and another, "I follow Apollos," are you not mere men?

What, after all, is Apollos? And what is Paul? Only servants, through whom you came to believe—as the Lord has assigned to each his task. I planted the seed, Apollos watered it, but God made it grow. (1 Corinthians 3:4–6)

Yet, at the same time, Paul, like the other apostles, knew he had to set a standard. He was required not only to preach but to embody the gospel, to live the kind of life others could emulate. He said so on several occasions:

Therefore I urge you to imitate me. (1 Corinthians 4:16)

Follow my example, as I follow the example of Christ. (1 Corinthians 11:1)

You became imitators of us and of the Lord. (1 Thessalonians 1:6)

Clearly, Paul viewed the Christian life as one of progress, and he felt duty-bound to "succeed" to such a degree that others could follow in his footsteps. The same reasoning underlies the entire teaching ministry of the church. You would not want to learn evangelism from a person who had never helped someone turn to Christ. You would not entrust your children to a Sunday school teacher who did not have a firm grasp of the Bible or tolerate a preacher who taught morality without applying it in his own life. You would feel cheated if a person who gave you guidance was not in some demonstrable sense farther down the road than you were.

God seems to have made us in such a way that we instinctively strive to achieve. We are driven by a basic, inner restlessness. Some devote their efforts to acquiring big houses, big cars, and big reputations. But, although God doesn't rule out prosperity (the promise of material reward is implicit in the Christian work ethic), the Bible makes clear that reputation and possessions can never satisfy the hunger within. Humankind's deepest need is spiritual. Whether we realize it or not, our striving is ultimately for wholeness in God.

WHAT SUCCESS LOOKS LIKE FROM HEAVEN

Success for the Christian, then, has nothing to do with things such as getting a private education for our children or boosting the size of our congregation. It is measured by the degree of our commitment to Jesus Christ and the determination with which we seek to satisfy that deep-seated hunger by saying, "More! Give me more of God!" To be called a successful Christian, I must be (to borrow the title of Oswald Chambers's classic book) giving "my utmost for His highest." That, I believe, is why the apostle Paul constantly urged believers to strive for spiritual growth.

The key to Christian success is this: *being unbending where it matters*. As Christians, we have plenty of room for flexibility and discretion. But there are certain points at which we must never give way, points at which there is simply no room for compromise. That has always been true for God's people.

During the time Samuel judged Israel, the Israelites demanded to have a king. Samuel would have rejected this request out of hand, but the Lord told him otherwise:

> *Listen to all that the people are saying to you; it is not you they have rejected, but they have rejected me as their king. As they have done from the day I brought them up out of Egypt until this day, forsaking me and serving other gods, so they are doing to you. Now listen to them; but warn them solemnly and let them know what the king who will reign over them will do. (1 Samuel 8:7–9)*

On this apparently crucial matter of principle, God required Samuel to be flexible. But He also made clear that this dangerous innovation of kingship in Israel must be bound in a ring of steel. So when the first king, Saul, flagrantly disobeyed God's command, Samuel took him to task:

> *"You have rejected the word of the Lord, and the Lord has rejected you as king over Israel!"*
> *As Samuel turned to leave, Saul caught hold of the hem of his*

robe, and it tore. Samuel said to him, "The Lord has torn the kingdom of Israel from you today and has given it to one of your neighbors—to one better than you." (1 Samuel 15:26–28)

It's a brave man who tells a king that his kingdom is to be snatched away from him. Yet Samuel did not hesitate. He was unbending where it mattered.

Centuries later Jesus was in the Garden of Gethsemane praying: "Father, if you are willing, take this cup from me; yet not my will, but yours be done" (Luke 22:42). Jesus knew that the path He was walking led to the cross. At almost any point in His life He could have stepped back and saved Himself. Indeed, at the start of His ministry, Satan tempted Him to do just that: "All this I will give you," Satan said, showing Jesus the kingdoms of the world, "if you will bow down and worship me" (Matthew 4:9). But Jesus knew that winning the victory for humankind meant enduring the pain. Success for Jesus meant obeying the will of the Father—even if it cost Him His life.

> *It's a rare and brave leader who stands up for what he believes when no one else in the world agrees with him.*

This absolute refusal to compromise on the key issues was a hallmark of Jesus' ministry. When He debated with the scribes and Pharisees, Jesus didn't take as His authority any rabbinical school or ancient tradition. He anchored His teaching on God's word alone. So authoritative was His teaching that His hearers frequently expressed amazement (see Mark 2:12). Jesus didn't try to be diplomatic. He did not go along to get along. Nor did He seek to win over His opponents by conceding to their demands. He was unbending where it mattered and unrelenting in His obedience to the Father.

ARTHRITIC CHRISTIANITY

Being "unbending" is not a prominent characteristic of our modern culture. If you want to frighten a political leader, all you have to do is accuse him of being a bigot or intolerant of others' viewpoints. To the liberal, intolerance is the ultimate faux pas. Convictions have flown out the window. It's a rare and brave leader who stands up for what he believes when no one else in the world agrees with him.

From coast to coast, in business, government, and homes, Americans do not do what is right but what is customary and popular. When the church stands up to the liberal ethos, it does so in a haphazard manner. Christians find it easy to be unbending, but they don't always understand what they should be unbending about. If you don't believe me, throw out a suggestion at your next annual meeting that your church change the style of its Sunday worship. You'll soon hear what one writer has called the Seven Last Words of the Church: "This is how we've always done it." Too often in the church, tradition rules the roost. People are unbending where it *doesn't* matter; they're not so much resolute as arthritic. But they're not the first.

> *One Sabbath Jesus was going through the grainfields, and as his disciples walked along, they began to pick some heads of grain. The Pharisees said to him, "Look, why are they doing what is unlawful on the Sabbath?"*
>
> *He answered, "Have you never read what David did when he and his companions were hungry and in need? In the days of Abiathar the high priest, he entered the house of God and ate the consecrated bread, which is lawful only for priests to eat. And he also gave some to his companions."*
>
> *Then he said to them, "The Sabbath was made for man, not man for the Sabbath. So the Son of Man is Lord even of the Sabbath." (Mark 2:23–28)*

To the Pharisees' kind of firmness, Jesus was implacably opposed. The Pharisees—the religious intellectuals of their day—had become so obsessed with razor-sharp distinctions in God's law that they'd forgotten why the law existed. They couldn't see the forest for the trees.

True, there was a principle to be observed here: that the Sabbath day had been set aside for rest. From the Pharisees' point of view, however, the principle could be made real only by applying it rigidly to scores of special cases. Consequently, they failed to see any significant difference in principle between a man harvesting a field and a man plucking a few heads of grain because he was hungry. On the Sabbath both actions were equally wrong. They seemed unaware that by applying the law in this way they brought the principle of Sabbath rest into conflict with the overall purpose of the law, which was to enhance human well-being. Abiathar the priest didn't withhold bread from David on the technicality of its having been consecrated. Human need puts the law in abeyance: the Sabbath is made for man, not man for the Sabbath.

In God's corporation there are always higher directives against which our firmness should be weighed—directives we all too quickly lose sight of. In His dealings with the Pharisees, Jesus reminds us of the dangers involved in applying policies blindly: "Woe to you, teachers of the law and Pharisees, you hypocrites! You give a tenth of your spices—mint, dill and cummin. But you have neglected the more important matters of the law—justice, mercy and faithfulness. You should have practiced the latter, without neglecting the former" (Matthew 23:23).

In all of this, the arbiter is the Word of God. If the Pharisees had returned to the Scriptures, they would have seen the purpose behind the principle: the true meaning of Sabbath rest. The Bible is the corporation's handbook, the standard to which everyone is asked to adhere. Those of us who have received the call of a lifetime are to be unbending in the things that *matter*, and those things are revealed to us by Scripture. What more famous example of this is there than the story of Martin Luther?

HERE I STAND

In 1521, the Reformer Martin Luther was summoned to a trial before Emperor Charles V. Luther had condemned the corruption of the church of Rome. He had denounced the sale of indulgences as a scam. And now the sky was falling on him. His books were being burned; Germany was being rent asunder by the emerging Reformation; and the newly proclaimed emperor, whose vast domains included staunchly Roman Spain, had nothing to gain by taking Luther's side against the pope.

Charles promised Luther safe conduct to the trial—hardly a guarantee of safety since the last rebel to have trusted himself to it, Jan Hus, ended up being burned at the stake. Luther, though, was determined to go.

When on April 16 he entered the city of Worms in a Saxon two-wheeled cart, no less than two thousand people turned out to conduct him to his lodgings. On the following day, he was brought to the court, where an official showed him a pile of books and asked whether they were his. Luther replied quietly, "The books are all mine, and I have written more."

"Do you defend them all, or do you care to reject a part?" the official asked.

So serious a question was this that it took until the next day for Luther to produce an answer. When he did so, however, the official remained unimpressed. "Martin," he said, "how can you assume that you are the only one to understand the sense of Scripture? Would you put your judgment above that of so many famous men and claim that you know more than they all? You have no right to call into question the most holy and orthodox faith, instituted by Christ the perfect law-giver, proclaimed throughout the world by the apostles, sealed by the red blood of the martyrs. . . . I ask you, Martin, candidly and without horns, do you or do you not repudiate your books and the errors which they contain?"

Faced with the possibility of arrest and execution, it would have been easy enough for Luther to back down, to equivocate, to reach an acceptable compromise. But he answered in these words: "Unless I am convicted by Scripture and plain reason . . . my conscience is captive to the Word of God. I cannot and I will not recant anything, for to go against conscience is neither right nor safe. Here I stand. I cannot do otherwise. God help me. Amen."

From that moment of courage and conviction sprang the Reformation. Notice what Luther said. He was bound to his conscience, and his conscience was informed by "Scripture and plain reason." Convinced—against the better judgment of the theologians—that the Bible meant exactly what it said, Luther had no choice but to dig in his heels. He was absolutely unbending, though he knew that other men had lost their lives for showing the same resolve.

Few of us will experience the kind of "defining moment" that confronted Luther at the Diet of Worms. Nevertheless, in our pursuit of Christian success we need to understand where and how to take our stand. And exactly the same principles apply.

SUCCESS STARTS HERE . . .

In the average corporation, the management structure itself reflects the "success" of the people on the payroll. Success is defined in terms of financial and social power, and thus the farther up you are on the corporate ladder, the more successful you are deemed to be.

From a Christian point of view, this arrangement has some obvious flaws. For one thing, can we call the executive with a broken marriage *successful* in any meaningful way? Surely success involves more than just income and influence. But, also, as soon as you move into God's corporation, the ground rules themselves change. The people who occupy the "senior management positions"—the clergy, and above them the moderators, bishops, famous evangelists—aren't necessarily the most "successful" in the sense we have given the word in this chapter. Measured against the scale of personal commitment, the church cleaning lady may be more successful than the minister.

> *In a culture that measures success*
> *by outward attainment, it's easy*
> *to forget that all gifts and abilities*
> *have equal value in God's economy.*

The peculiar temptations to which ministry is prone—including pride and complacency—can form a serious impediment to the degree of success achieved by those we call church leaders. After all, what qualifies Jesus to occupy the chairman's seat isn't power or experience; it's a record of redemptive suffering and obedience to the will of the Father. As we search for success as Christians, therefore, we would do well to remember the following points.

1. God's work begins with grace. Nobody has head-hunted us. We didn't come into the church as winning candidates off a shortlist. It's one of the peculiarities of God's corporation that He selects the most unpromising employees from the least likely backgrounds. We have no ground for pride. As Paul reminds the Corinthians, "Not many of you were wise by human standards; not many were influential; not many were of noble birth. But God chose the foolish things of the world to shame the wise" (1 Corinthians 1:26–27). Whatever we had when we entered our new life with Christ and whatever we have acquired since have come to us only by God's grace. If I can paint like Rembrandt, drive like Michael Schumacher, or sing like Caruso, I am not entitled to congratulate myself. Instead, I should give thanks to God.

2. We all have the resources for Christian success. The capacity for faithfulness, so essential to Christian commitment, has been given to all of us. That doesn't mean that it's easy to perfect. Brush aside the superficial thinking our century has attached to the word *success*, and we find such powerful concepts as reliability, trustworthiness, dependability, devotion, authenticity, loyalty, credibility, resolve, steadfastness, constancy, dedication. All of these contribute to the virtue of faithfulness. And we are all equally challenged by them.

3. Not everyone succeeds in the same way. In a well-known passage, Paul wrote, "There are different kinds of gifts, but the same Spirit. There are different kinds of service, but the same Lord. There are different kinds of working, but the same God works all of them in all men. Now to each one the manifestation of the Spirit is given for the common good" (1 Corinthians 12:4–7). In a culture that measures success by outward attainment, it's easy to forget that all gifts and abilities have equal value in God's economy. God has endowed some with unusual, even supernatural, abilities against which others can look fairly mundane. But "spiritual gifts" are still gifts. The ability to converse in five languages and to work in a demanding overseas position is no more (and no less) commendable in God's eyes than vacuuming the church floor or encouraging the fainthearted. Nor is the task of preaching the sermon on a Sunday morning to be considered any more noble than the task of sitting in the pews and listening to it. Every job in God's corporation needs doing. And by God's grace every person is uniquely qualified for a particular role.

4. You are a spiritual bridgehead. In a sense, God depends on us to achieve His work in the world. The less success we achieve in Christian terms, therefore, the less God is able to do through us. We are spiritual bridgeheads in enemy territory; we need to expand so that God can pour more resources into us and make us more effective. That doesn't mean we all become famous—there was only one Paul, one Martin Luther, one John Wesley—but becoming famous isn't a mark of success from the Christian point of view. What matters is to find the position God has called us to in His corporation and then to do our job to the best of our ability so that, over the years ahead, He can use us to the limits of our potential.

4

CONFRONTATION:

Speak the Truth—and Be True

Imagine walking into a shop where they sell religion. You've got plenty of choices. You can have any kind of religion, just as in a clothing store you can buy any kind of shirt. Christianity, Islam, Buddhism, Hinduism—all the big-name brands are there, plus lots of smaller ones you've probably never heard of. So you pick some up, try them on for size, and eventually go to the sales clerk with something called Protestant Christianity.

"Very popular model," the sales clerk observes. "A lot of people go for that one."

"But is it true?" you ask. "You see, I particularly want a religion that's *true.*"

"Of course it's true," replies the sales clerk. "Look at the tag line."

So you look at the tag line under the manufacturer's name, and you see that it says *Christianity: the Way, the Truth, the Life.*

You find this reassuring. "So this is the one true religion, and all the rest are false," you say.

But the sales clerk looks shocked. "Oh no," she insists. "They're *all* true . . ."

By now, I expect, you've seen the crack in the logic. Truth isn't the kind of thing you can spread around thinly so that everybody has a little bit. A religion is either true or false, just like the testimony of a witness is either true or false. If you say "I believe in God very strongly, but I realize I may be wrong," you are really saying nothing at all. What use is it if a witness stands up in court and says, "I believe I saw the defendant rob the bank, but of course it could have been somebody else"?

This is distinctly *not* the tone of the Bible. At least twice in the opening chapter of his gospel, John describes Jesus Christ unequivocally and uncompromisingly as "the truth." First, in John 1:14 he tells us that Jesus was full of grace and truth. Then in verse 17 he says that grace and truth found their ultimate fulfillment in Jesus Christ. This truth, he later says, "will set you free" (John 8:32).

Modern Americans enjoy a lot of freedom. They are free from foreign domination. They are free from the fear of conflict between the superpowers. They are free from the threat of communism. They are free, within the limits of the Constitution, to do and say as they wish, without fear of reprisal from the state. At a deeper level, and thanks to the grace of God, they are free, as every human being is, to choose Christ as their Savior or to reject Him.

But that freedom to choose, though God-given, is not the same as the freedom to *live*. When Jesus said, "The truth shall make you free," He meant that there is only one belief with the power to liberate and transform. You can choose as much as you like, but unless your choosing brings you to the truth, it will do you no good whatever.

IS TRUTH RELATIVE?

We should understand just how far this idea of truth differs from the democratic idea common in society around us. To the modern Western mind-set, all truth is relative. Your truth and my truth may be different, but they weigh exactly the same. Outside the realm of demonstrable fact, there is (at least officially) no such thing as one person's view being more valid than another's. In a world populated solely by the blind, opinions as to what the world actually looks like are deemed equal.

The idea of relativism came partly from the German

philosopher Immanuel Kant. Kant's assertion—that no one can ever know objective truth—used to be the kind of dry philosophical proposition discussed only among university professors. No longer. It has found arms and legs and is now running rampant from Main Street to Wall Street— even in our elementary schools.

There is, writes Allan Bloom in *The Closing of the American Mind*, "one thing a professor can be absolutely certain of: almost every student entering the university believes, or says he believes, that truth is relative." We are allowed to say, pretty much what we like—except what, as Christians, we know to be right. Real truth is off-limits. I know that because my own children have been taught by people who have fallen into this error. They profess to value the truth (in the sense of "being honest with oneself and others"), but, if someone speaks from Christian convictions, they become aggressive and narrow-minded.

Ninety-one percent of Americans lie on a regular basis.

Fifteen years have taught me that much the same happens in many mainline churches. If any institution stands for absolute and unflinching truth, it should be the church. Yet relativism is alive and well in the clergy meeting, just as it is everywhere else in America. I remember putting forward the view that Jesus embodied the whole and undiluted truth and that no other religion or school of thought possessed the same fullness of truth we find in Christ. I was howled down. I got accused of narrow-mindedness, stubbornness, and lack of charity. But in the same meeting feminists who spoke of "Sophia" as the goddess of wisdom were applauded for their willingness to seek truth and to be open to new ideas. The implication appears to be that seeking for truth is admirable—so long as you never find it.

WHY AMERICANS LIE

Jim Patterson and Peter Kim, in their book *The Day America Told the Truth*, made the astounding claim that 91 percent of Americans lie on a regular basis. Telling lies and believing in the relativity of truth are intimately connected. In a society where so-called Christian theological schools no longer regard Jesus Christ as the full and only embodiment of truth, it's hardly surprising to find truth devalued at the level of day-to-day interaction. Lying becomes routine.

The Day America Told the Truth contains some fascinating insights about who lies to whom—assuming, of course, that you can trust its sources:

- The unemployed lie more than those who have a job.
- The poor lie more than the rich.
- Liberals lie more than conservatives.
- Gays and bisexuals lie more than heterosexuals.
- Young men lie more than older men.
- Men lie more than women.

Naturally, the reasons people tell lies are many and complex, and probably most people, most of the time, don't lie out of malice the way the serpent did when he tempted Eve. More often they lie out of fear. They're aware of a "truth-gap" between their actions and the expectations of others around them, so they lie to protect themselves from criticism, rejection, ridicule, or punishment. The businessman dating his secretary tells his wife he had to work late. The politician who "adjusted" his taxes blames the mistake on his accountants. And so on.

Incidentally, the people whose criticism you fear aren't always in the right. I can recall, as a youngster, lying to the Franciscan nuns who taught me and being told in return that I'd have my tongue cut out with a razor. I realize now that they had no intention of carrying out the threat, which means, of course, that they were trying to cure me of lying by lying themselves—something with which the clinical psychologists would have a field day.

Whether those around you are right or wrong, however, the effect is the same. If you know that the truth is unpalatable, you feel strongly tempted to cover it up. Imagine the pressure that must have been on Jesus when Pilate asked him, "Are you the king of the Jews?" (John 18:33). The suspicion that Jesus claimed to be the Messiah was exactly what led the Jews to seek His execution. To deny the claim before Pilate—who wasn't known for his Jewish sympathies anyway—would have opened a handy escape hatch from crucifixion. Very likely Pilate would have seen Jesus as an innocent persecuted by religious fanatics and simply let Him go. But Jesus didn't take the easy way out:

> Jesus said, "My kingdom is not of this world. If it were, my servants would fight to prevent my arrest by the Jews. But now my kingdom is from another place."
> "You are a king, then!" said Pilate.
> Jesus answered, "You are right in saying I am a king. In fact, for this reason I was born, and for this I came into the world, to testify to the truth. Everyone on the side of truth listens to me."
> "What is truth?" Pilate asked. (John 18:36–38)

Jesus knew that telling the truth about Himself would lead directly to His execution. Yet He didn't flinch from telling it. Pilate, purposely not pursuing a discussion with Jesus on the nature of truth, was forced to confront the Jews armed with nothing more than his own opinion of Jesus' innocence.

ASK NO QUESTIONS, HEAR NO LIES?

The Christian church is—or should be—the one place in which the truth can be told and heard without pretense. But, instead of fostering a climate of truth-telling and repentance and forgiveness, we have fudged the truth issue and turned a blind eye to wrongdoing. We neglect to challenge each other, so truth goes by the board.

To be sure, truth in the church is a delicate issue. I went through a tough time in my early days in the pastorate, confronting people with what I believed was the truth about their lifestyles. I learned the hard way that they could not handle the truth-gap. Rather than dealing with their errors, they simply checked out of the church. On some occasions I literally pleaded with them; I implored them with tears to repent and assured them of my willingness to help in the search for restoration. But it was to no avail. The stigma of being "found out," of having their shortcomings brought out into the open, far outweighed the benefits of confession and repentance.

Now there *ought* to be no need for rebuke in the Christian community. Christians *ought* to understand and implement gospel teaching, and as a result they *ought* to have no guilty secrets. The Truth that lives in them *ought* to shine out consistently and transparently. There *ought* to be no shadows, no dark corners.

But those of us who have responded to the call of a lifetime aren't perfect. We're not yet sitting in the heavenly mansion, and, despite all our good intentions, we sin and make mistakes. The truth is, we are sinners for whom Christ died, and our redemption doesn't automatically keep us from sinning. For that reason, those who think they sin less should hesitate before rebuking those they think sin more.

That's not to say, however, that truth is unattainable. There *is* a standard against which we are all measured, and the fact that none of us rates 100 percent shouldn't stop us striving together to improve or encouraging one another in our efforts. When Jesus is in the executive suite, the corporate policy is clear and the standards high.

So how should truth be handled?

THE ANTIOCH CASE

Although a Jew himself, Paul quickly took on board the radical new "corporate policy" of preaching salvation to everyone. But in this respect Paul was unusual: most of the other Jewish Christians found it difficult to shake off their separatist spirit. After all, it was customary for Jews to refer to outsiders as "dogs."

The Background

The controversy came to a head at the Council of Jerusalem (Acts 15). By that time Paul and Barnabas had already completed their first missionary journey to the Gentiles, and Peter had already understood, through a heavenly vision, that God meant to push the boundaries of His kingdom way beyond the bounds of Israel.

At Jerusalem, Peter recounted again how God had led him to baptize the first Gentile believers, concluding firmly, "We believe it is through the grace of our Lord Jesus that we are saved, just as they are" (verse 11). After this, Paul and Barnabas confirmed that this directive from God had resulted in miraculous conversions among the Gentiles on their first missionary journey (verse 12). Finally, James spoke, the man most now believe to have been the pastor of the Jerusalem church:

> *"Brothers, listen to me. Simon [Peter] has described to us how God at first showed his concern by taking from the Gentiles a people for himself. The words of the prophets are in agreement with this, as it is written:*
>> *"'After this I will return*
>>> *and rebuild David's fallen tent.*
>> *Its ruins I will rebuild,*
>>> *and I will restore it,*
>> *that the remnant of men may seek the Lord,*
>>> *and all the Gentiles who bear my name,*
>> *says the Lord, who does these things'*
>>> *that have been known for ages.*
>
> *"It is my judgment, therefore, that we should not make it difficult for the Gentiles who are turning to God." (verses 13–19)*

As a kind of token requirement, James cited four things the Gentiles should abstain from: (1) Food polluted by idols (that is, food previously sacrificed to idols—a theme developed by Paul in 1 Corinthians 8). (2) Sexual immorality, or unchastity. This referred both to general sexual promiscuity and also to what was known as "sacred" prostitution in heathen cults. (3) Meat from strangulated animals—a delicacy in pagan society. (4) Consumption of blood. This may have been a corollary of the previous restriction, strangulation being specifically forbidden in the Jewish law because "the life . . . is in the blood" (Leviticus 17:11; see 3:17; Deuteronomy 12:23–25). No objections to James's proposal are recorded by Luke, and the council went on to draft a letter that would circulate the agreement among the churches.

The four points appear to have been the ones most vigorously contested between the Jewish and Gentile Christians. It could be asked, of course, why the church failed to embrace what, in retrospect, was clearly the "true gospel." As I interpret Acts 15, James offered what was revealed to him by the Holy Spirit: namely, a bridge of contact between two distinctive religious cultures, which included the critical concession from Jewish believers that Gentiles should be exempted from circumcision. At any rate, the true gospel soon asserted itself. It is significant that, of the four instructions issued from Jerusalem, the only one to survive concerned sexual immorality (an ongoing concern, as the first epistle to the Corinthians shows). The other three, all of which were rooted in Jewish ideas of ritual cleanness, are never heard again.

Paul had no need of such stepping-stones away from Jewish faith. Once he had grasped the concept of grace, he never let it go. Consequently, for the most part it is through Paul's inspired understanding that we see the significance of God's incarnation in Jesus Christ:

> *But now in Christ Jesus you who once were far away have been brought near through the blood of Christ.*
>
> *For he himself is our peace, who has made the two one and has destroyed the barrier, the dividing wall of hostility, by abolishing in his flesh the law with its commandments and regulations. His purpose was to create in himself one new man out of the two, thus making peace, and in this one body to reconcile both of them to God through the cross. (Ephesians 2:13–16)*

> *You are all sons of God through faith in Christ Jesus, for all of you who were baptized into Christ have clothed yourselves with*

Christ. There is neither Jew nor Greek, slave nor free, male nor female, for you are all one in Christ Jesus. If you belong to Christ, then you are Abraham's seed, and heirs according to the promise. (Galatians 3:26–29)

It's hard for us today to see just how radical Paul's thinking was to a church that still regarded itself in some sense as Jewish. The Jews of the period were used to having religious Gentiles in their worship services; but to acknowledge that in God's view Jews and Gentiles were *equal* was a paradigm shift. After all, they must have argued, the dietary code had been given to them through the inspired Scriptures (see Leviticus 11 and Deuteronomy 14). For hundreds of years, faithful Jews had resisted absorption by paganism. They held dearly the things that made them different—circumcision, ceremonial cleansing, and kosher observances—because these formed the backbone of their faith.

The Details

Against such a background, then, did Paul confront Peter in Antioch. The event is not recorded in Acts, but it rests on the same dispute that gave rise to the Jerusalem Council. One party in the church—largely Jewish—believed that Christians should adhere closely to Jewish customs; the other—largely Gentile—was unfamiliar with Jewish customs and saw little reason for preserving them.

For Paul it was clearly a matter of making policy stick. The church was God's new organization, emerging into a new world. It could not afford to carry with it the trappings of another, older faith. "This matter arose because some false brothers had infiltrated our ranks to spy on the freedom we have in Christ Jesus and to make us slaves. We did not give in to them for a moment, so that the truth of the gospel might remain with you" (Galatians 2:4–5). The principle was so important that Paul had to stand firm, no matter who opposed him:

When Peter came to Antioch, I opposed him to his face, because he was clearly in the wrong. Before certain men came from James, he used to eat with the Gentiles. But when they arrived, he began to draw back and separate himself from the Gentiles because he was afraid of those who belonged to the circumcision group. The other Jews joined him in his hypocrisy, so that by their hypocrisy even Barnabas was led astray.

When I saw that they were not acting in line with the truth of the gospel, I said to Peter in front of them all, "You are a Jew, yet you live like a Gentile and not like a Jew. How is it, then, that you force Gentiles to follow Jewish customs?

"We who are Jews by birth and not 'Gentile sinners' know that a man is not justified by observing the law, but by faith in Jesus Christ. So we, too, have put our faith in Christ Jesus that we may be justified by faith in Christ and not by observing the law, because by observing the law no one will be justified." (Galatians 2:11–16)

That it was Peter who erred made matters all the worse. After all, in God's corporation he was an executive board member, someone others looked to as their example. Paul's charge that Peter "was clearly in the wrong" (verse 11) has been translated in various ways:

"was to be blamed" (NKJV)
"stood condemned" (NAS; RSV)
"stood self-condemned" (NRSV)
"was manifestly in the wrong" (JB)
"was very wrong" (TLB)

The differences indicate the difficulty translators have had in communicating; the force of the rebuke. Peter was more than just wrong; he was also inconsistent and deceitful. If he really stood by the Jewish law, he shouldn't have eaten with Gentiles, even when there were no Jewish believers there to see him, for age-old regulations prevented Jews from eating with "pagans." If he really stood for the inclusion of the Gentiles—which he claimed to do at the Council of Jerusalem—he shouldn't have spurned the company of Gentile Christians at Antioch.

MAKING THE TRUTH COUNT

We can learn a number of lessons from the way Paul confronted Peter.

1. He Dealt with Truth Face-to-Face

Paul didn't take the coward's way out. He didn't spread malicious gossip behind Peter's back. He didn't register a complaint with the other apostles and try to get Peter ousted. He talked to Peter man to man.

2. He Used a Public Rebuke to Deal with a Public Act

Not all rebukes need to be delivered under the glare of spotlights. Many are far better dealt with on a private basis. But so important was the issue here that it could not be resolved quietly behind closed doors. Paul knew that Peter, the chief of all the apostles, was guilty of duplicity, and he met this public failure with a public rebuke. Without that, it would have been far harder to clear the air. After all, this wasn't just about Peter; it was about the whole church. Paul wanted a public acknowledgment that corporate policy was right.

3. He Rebuked the Action, Not the Person

It's important not to let an argument about one particular issue spill over into other unrelated areas. A rebuke that gets personal has been ill-conceived. Paul had no intention of toppling Peter. No power struggle existed between the two leaders. Both had their separate spheres of service— Peter to the Jews and Paul to the Gentiles. If Paul hadn't believed Peter to be badly—disastrously—in the wrong, he wouldn't have had the temerity to stage a showdown.

4. He Acknowledged the Scale of Peter's Accomplishments

This was no demolition job. When Paul said to Peter, "You are a Jew, yet you live like a Gentile and not like a Jew," he paid Peter a richly deserved compliment. It is a much more liberated Peter we see here than we see in the Gospels. We learn in Acts that God first used Peter to preach to the Gentiles at the home of a Roman soldier, Cornelius. Peter was able to say in his report to the Jerusalem leaders,

"As I began to speak, the Holy Spirit came on them as he had come on us at the beginning. Then I remembered what the Lord had said: 'John baptized with water, but you will be baptized with the Holy Spirit.' So if God gave them the same gift as he gave us, who believed in the Lord Jesus Christ, who was I to think that I could oppose God?" (Acts 11:15–17)

A leader will often assume that he is right and everyone else is wrong.

It was in exactly this spirit that Peter conducted himself when he first arrived in Antioch, mixing freely and happily with the Gentile believers. Only when messengers from Jerusalem arrived did the fear introduce itself into Peter's mind: What would his "home crowd" make of his liberated behavior? Fear turned itself into a lie. Whatever he *said* about relations between the Jewish and Gentile believers, Peter's *actions* told everyone that Jewish scruples came before Gentile freedom. He was, in a sense, a victim of his own narrow experience. It took Paul, coming from outside the select group of apostles, to see the implications of Jesus' "mission statement": "Whoever comes to me I will never drive away" (John 6:37).

5. He Didn't Get Carried Away with Self-importance

Paul wrote, "By the grace given me I say to every one of you: Do not think of yourself more highly than you ought, but rather think of yourself with sober judgment" (Romans 12:3). It is a besetting sin among leaders that they think of themselves too highly. When he's offended or angered or under stress, a leader will often assume that he is right and everyone else is wrong. Not only that, but he'll often get annoyed at others for not living up to his own strict standards.

There is no evidence of this in Paul's rebuke to Peter. Nor can it be found in Jesus' treatment of His own disciples in the Garden of Gethsemane: "When he came back, he again found them sleeping, because their eyes were heavy" (Matthew 26:43). If ever anyone had a right to be annoyed, it was Jesus then and there. After three years of exhausting ministry Jesus was about to be arrested and killed, but all that his friends could do was snore. Jesus did not shake them or shout at them. He knew they had reached the end of their endurance, and He accepted it. "So he left them and went away once more and prayed" (verse 44).

6. He Decided Which Principles Came First

Paul did not hesitate to put the principle of truth before the principle of peace. Fear made Peter do the opposite: he sacrificed truth so as not to incur criticism. But in God's organization you've got to be able to judge when principles should take second place to human needs. When Paul rebuked Peter over his change of behavior, he was doing more than expressing a difference of opinion. The whole edifice of New Testament theology was built on the principle Paul stood for. It was, if you like, the corporate ethos of the church. If Paul had let it slip—if he'd said, in effect, that believers still needed to meet some of the law's requirements in order to be saved—he would have undermined the entire organization. The lesser principles that the Jewish Christians observed as a matter of personal piety had to give way before the greater principle of salvation by faith alone. No question about it. If Paul had not ranked his principles in this way, we might still be requiring circumcision as a mark of entry into God's kingdom.

SUMMING UP

When Jesus is in the executive suite, truth matters. We cannot treat it casually. We are called upon as Christians to live consistently on the basis of clear principles. If we do so, we have nothing to fear. Nothing that another person can say to us, no revelation about our private life, can ever cause us embarrassment or shame.

But because we continue to make mistakes and take the coward's way out by covering up, it is necessary for Christians to correct one another. Anyone in management will be confronted regularly with situations where it is necessary to correct, discipline, and remotivate an employee. In all this, Christ's directives on living the truth are far from being a carte blanche for character assassination. The controls on the person who corrects another are strong. And leaders are certainly not permitted to rebuke anyone with whom they happen to disagree. Perhaps the underlying principle to be gleaned from the Gospels is that—if we can possibly do so—we should find ways of dealing with differences without outright confrontation. "A gentle answer," as the proverb says, "turns away wrath" (Proverbs 15:1).

5

RESPONSIBILITY:

People Who Drive Need a Destination

There's a science fiction story about a group of students from a survival class who are taking their final exam. Each student is ferried to an unknown planet and abandoned there with nothing to protect him or her but wits and a single weapon. Those who were still alive after twelve months made the grade.

Before they left, they had their choice of weapons. Almost everyone took the most sophisticated rifle, plus several boxes of ammunition. The main character in the story was about to follow suit when an old professor laid a hand on his shoulder. "The gun is too heavy," the professor said, "and it will make you overconfident. I advise you to take only a hunting knife." Though doubtful, the student accepted this advice. After a year on the mystery planet, surrounded by dinosaurs, he was one of the few in his class left alive.

The story, of course, has a moral behind it: Choose wisely if you want to do well. Becoming an adult is really a process of taking responsibility for our choices. Every choice we make opens one door and leaves others closed. And our choices of which doors in life to open largely define who we are.

My life, which began in Egypt, has been dominated by several big decisions, of which the most important by far was the decision to become a Christian. That was a serious choice to make in a predominantly Muslim country, even though my parents belonged to the church. But I heard God calling me, and I opened the door and went through. I've made other important decisions too: to leave the nation of my birth, to study, to marry, to immigrate to the United States, to make a major career shift into ordained ministry. On each occasion I heard God calling me, and I decided to obey. That's how I've grown. That's how I've become who I am.

Now the phrase "I heard God calling me" can be misleading. I have never been awakened in the middle of the night like the young Samuel to have God's will explained to me in plain English. That God is calling us to do a certain thing is a conviction we reach prayerfully, and often slowly, through an examination of our talents, desires, ambitions, motives, attitudes, responsibilities, and options. The process isn't perfect or foolproof—that would be too much to expect—but in my experience that's how it works.

> *The one who says "if only" isn't taking responsibility for the troubles or heartbreaks or struggles in his or her life.*

And remember this: *We* are the ones who make the decision. God may urge us toward a certain door, but *we* open it. Others may put pressure on us to follow a certain route along life's highway, but *we* drive the car. If we deny that, we have to see ourselves either as robots being made to scurry around by some supernatural radio-control device or as weak-minded individuals without the guts to chart our own course. Thus, when things go wrong, we blame others—bad luck or inept advisers. Instead of taking responsibility for our lives, we perpetually look back at what we suppose to be irredeemably bad decisions and say, "It wasn't my fault."

It's not hard to tell when somebody's life has gone out of control like this, because their conversation fills up with "if onlys": "If only my wife/husband had encouraged me . . .";

"If only my parents hadn't forced me to . . ."; "If only my boss would . . ." The list goes on. The one who says "if only" isn't taking responsibility for the troubles or heartbreaks or struggles in his or her life.

Of course, that's not to deny the impact outside events can make. I can sympathize with a person who says, "If only my child didn't have leukemia" or "If only that tornado hadn't devastated my business." To some extent, many of the things that happen to us lie outside our control. But to a large extent many of them also fall within the sweep of our decision making and influence.

You would think that your rate of recovery after an illness would depend mostly on the severity of the condition and the quality of the medical care—things you have no control over. But research indicates that patients whose rooms overlook a park or a river recover faster than those without such a view. In some way, the active, wide-awake world beyond the window calls to them and reminds them of the need to get back on their feet.

Even if your illness is terminal, your control over it remains substantial. Hospital personnel will tell you that the terminally ill frequently choose their moment of death. They hold on for as long as it takes for some goal to be reached—the arrival of a distant loved one, the completion of an important piece of work—and once that goal is attained, as often as not, they die within hours.

As employees in God's corporation, then, we are not called to be passive, allowing ourselves to be blown around by every wind of change. We are executives: we execute decisions, take initiatives. And the opportunities to do this confront us every day. So how do we decide well?

HOW YOU CHOOSE REVEALS YOUR VALUES

Rob, the pastor of a growing church in southern California, frequently reminded his congregation of the importance of putting Jesus first. Those who knew him would have said that Rob's values centered on absolute commitment to God. Nothing—not even family—came before his duty to Jesus Christ. As he often quoted, "If anyone comes to me and does not hate his father and mother, his wife and children, his brothers and sisters—yes, even his own life— he cannot be my disciple" (Luke 14:26).

One day Rob's six-year-old daughter ran into the street toward an ice cream vendor's truck and was hit by a speeding car. For two days she lay in a coma. The accident happened on a Friday afternoon. Sunday morning Rob didn't show up in his pulpit. In fact, he didn't preach for the next three weeks.

The point isn't that Rob failed to live up to his own exacting standards—I believe it was right for him to stay in the hospital—but that, when the moment of decision came, his *actual* values were not the ones he professed. His love for his family came higher on his order of priorities than his commitment to the church.

Thankfully, we don't all have our inconsistencies exposed in such a dire fashion. But actions do speak louder than words, and the decisions we make as members of God's corporation reveal a bewildering array of motives: we fail to keep a commitment because we "need a rest"; we compromise in order not to hurt another person's feelings; we go against our better judgment because we fear becoming unpopular. In fact, the decisions we make reveal so many conflicting urges that it may be difficult to identify anything resembling a coherent system of values. We really don't know what matters.

The first task in good decision making is to sort out the chain of command. Who is making your decisions? The Bible helps us indirectly here in its teaching about giving. After all, our giving involves a number of related decisions: how much, how often, who to—and whether we bother in the first place. Here is Paul's advice:

> *Remember this: Whoever sows sparingly will also reap sparingly, and whoever sows generously will also reap generously. Each man should give what he has decided in his heart to give, not reluctantly or under compulsion, for God loves a cheerful giver. And God is able to make all grace abound to you, so that in all things at all*

*times, having all that you need, you will abound in every good
work. As it is written:*

"*He has scattered abroad his gifts to the poor;
        his righteousness endures forever.*"

*Now he who supplies seed to the sower and bread for food will also
supply and increase your store of seed and will enlarge the harvest
of your righteousness. (2 Corinthians 9:6–10)*

Apparently the Corinthians had not learned to give help
to other Christians. Possibly they sensed a risk in giving
and feared that if they gave generously they'd suffer for it.
Paul assured them that God would prosper the generous
and enable them to give more. He also made clear that the
rewards of giving come in proportion to one's generosity:
The bag you use to carry your gifts is the same one you use
to carry your rewards.

But note this: Each was to give what he had decided "in
his heart to give, not reluctantly or under compulsion." The
form of the verb (the Greek middle voice) emphasizes a
personalized choice. Paul is saying, "Never mind what the
next person gives; what you give is your choice."

This is conspicuously unlike the kind of giving and the
kind of decision making that we are used to. Few of us can
manage to listen to our own hearts. We're far too conscious
of what others expect of us. Instead of making our own
decisions, we allow ourselves to be directed by other people's opinions, other people's desires, other people's values.
We want to please our peers. We don't want to look stingy.
So powerfully are some individuals influenced by others
that they even make major decisions—over jobs, housing,
marriage—against their better judgment.

Whenever this happens a dislocation appears between
people's values and their behavior. They are no longer inte-
grated beings but are expressing another's system of values.
They are acting under compulsion, and this compulsion
has stolen away their freedom. Subconsciously they know
this. Often they feel put-upon, resentful, taken advantage
of.

To choose well, therefore, it is essential to take responsibility for choosing. Certainly you may decide in favor of another person's (your wife's, your child's, your employer's) interests, but you must do this positively and not out of a fear of censure.

Two men were offered promotions involving relocation. Neither wife wanted to move, since this would mean disruption for the children, loss of friends, and giving up their own employment. Both couples talked their situations through, and both decided to relocate. But whereas the first wife made her objections known and said, "This isn't convenient for me, but I'm willing to make the sacrifice," the second gave way immediately because she didn't want to "make life difficult" for her husband.

Which was the better decision? I would say the first wife's, for, unlike the second, she faced up to all the consequences—not only the consequences for her situation but for her future state of mind. She counted the cost before she made the commitment; she counted the bricks before building the tower.

LOOK AT THE LAST DOMINO

Dean's church, started in 1908, reached its peak in the late 1940s with more than a thousand members. Originally the church was located in an affluent neighborhood in Atlanta. By 1960, however, the upper-middle-class professionals had moved out to the new suburbs, making way for an influx of blue-collar blacks and Hispanics. With only the elderly members remaining in the vicinity, membership plummeted to less than two hundred, and the congregation began to discuss selling the property and moving away.

Strangely, at this point a number of former members started returning to worship. "My parents were married and buried in this church," said one man. Others spoke of their emotional identification with the church. Over the year it took to sell the property and relocate, inactive members showed up regularly. One of them was Dean.

"I didn't know how much this place meant to me," he said, "until I realized we were going to lose it." The loss of the church building got him thinking. He wondered why he had such an affection for the place. He thought of his younger days—being baptized, joining the church, being married there—and realized he had lost something important in life. As a result, he became active in another church. "Until I faced the loss of the old building, I never knew how much my faith meant."

Long ago, Dean had made a choice. His choice was to move out of the church. What he hadn't done was to look at the line of dominoes leading away from that decision and finding out where it went. Only when he discovered that declining membership forced the closure of the old church building did it occur to him that his decision had consequences. His absence from the church had contributed to its decline. More important, though, it had sent his own life running in a wrong and unhealthy direction.

This willingness to predict consequences is a quality God requires of those who have been called to a lifetime of service in His corporation:

> *Therefore everyone who hears these words of mine and puts them into practice is like a wise man who built his house on the rock. The rain came down, the streams rose, and the winds blew and beat against that house; yet it did not fall, because it had its foundation on the rock. But everyone who hears these words of mine and does not put them into practice is like a foolish man who built his house on sand. The rain came down, the streams rose, and the winds blew and beat against that house, and it fell with a great crash. (Matthew 7:24–27)*

We can imagine several reasons why the foolish man would build his house on sand—it took less effort to dig the foundation, and he had fewer steps to climb to the front door. But these short-term advantages should have been measured against the long-term risk of having his investment washed away in a flood. A similar thing is taught in the parable of the wise and foolish virgins (see Matthew 25:1–13). The foolish virgins neglected to bring extra supplies of oil, so they had to go shopping at exactly the

moment the bridegroom's party arrived. In both stories the
fault is lack of foresight.

Much the same failure to think through the domino line
of consequences can be seen in divorce. During my time in
the ministry I have met many men and women who, after,
say, fifteen years of marriage, begin to grow restless with
each other (more men, it must be said, than women) and
decide that the answer to their problems is a divorce. They
seem to view marriage as equivalent to car ownership. If
the old model no longer suits them, they trade it in and get
a new one.

But it doesn't take a Ph.D. in psychology to understand
that relationships can't just be disposed of. After fifteen
years a spouse becomes part of you. There may be children
whose welfare will weigh heavily into the equation, circles
of friends who will have to absorb the shock of your ending
one relationship and starting another. Rationalizations
along the lines of "God wants me to be happy" just don't
wash in the rough-and-tumble of real life. Since when did
God want us to be egocentrically, selfishly, and unremit-
tingly *happy?*

In such situations our values show up not only as different from God's but as self-centered and petty. *We* may see
personal happiness as the top priority, but God takes the
wider view. Almost any modern person reading the New
Testament, for instance, will be struck by the fact that the
apostle Paul did not oppose slavery outright. He did not
commend it either; but the degree of liberty the slave
enjoyed in the particular form of slavery practiced in the
Roman world seemed to Paul less important than the way
in which slave and master treated each other. It was to this
issue, rather than to the ethics of slavery itself, that Paul
addressed himself:

> *Slaves, obey your earthly masters with respect and fear, and*
> *with sincerity of heart, just as you would obey Christ. Obey them*
> *not only to win their favor when their eye is on you, but like slaves*
> *of Christ, doing the will of God from your heart. Serve wholeheart-*
> *edly, as if you were serving the Lord, not men, because you know*

*that the Lord will reward everyone for whatever good he does,
whether he is slave or free.*

*And masters, treat your slaves in the same way. Do not threat-
en them, since you know that he who is both their Master and yours
is in heaven, and there is no favoritism with him. (Ephesians
6:5–9)*

Don't get me wrong—it's not that God doesn't like to see
us enjoying ourselves. But God's will doesn't lead inex-
orably toward the most enjoyable option. *Sometimes* it
leads somewhere very different.

I have said before that Jesus could have backed out of
His earthly mission at any time—He had that option. Usually we think of the great temptation as coming at the start
of His ministry, when Satan showed Him all the kingdoms
of the world and offered Him an easy way to power. But
even after forty days without food, I'm not sure that this
prospect was as alluring as when Jesus faced His crucifixion in the Garden of Gethsemane. At that point excruciat-
ing death was only hours away.

And not just crucifixion. What made Calvary peculiarly
painful to Jesus was the isolation it imposed. Jesus wasn't
the first martyr to be crucified, and He could have faced
His execution as courageously as the rest. He sweat blood
in the Garden of Gethsemane not for fear of physical pain
but because the sin He carried as a substitute for the
human race would—for the first time—cut Him off from
His Father. During the crucifixion, and in a paradox that
defies mortal logic, God would be unable to accept Him. He
would be broken. And it was the agony of this breaking that
made Jesus cry, "My God, my God, why have you forsaken
me?" (Matthew 27:46).

*Consistency is drawing a straight line
between your values and your actions—
and making sure everyone else can see it.*

Our humanity prevents us from grasping, even in outline, how terrible a choice this was for Jesus—what a forbidding door He was asked to open. His every instinct must have clamored against it. Yet that choice, and that choice alone, led to the Resurrection, the Ascension, and the salvation of the human race. "He humbled himself and became obedient to death—even death on a cross! Therefore God exalted him to the highest place and gave him the name that is above every name" (Philippians 2:8–9).

And the writer to the Hebrews exhorts us: "Let us fix our eyes on Jesus, the author and perfecter of our faith, who for the joy set before him endured the cross, scorning its shame, and sat down at the right hand of the throne of God" (Hebrews 12:2). Jesus had His eyes fixed on that last domino.

BE CONSISTENT

Like Jesus, we need consistency. I don't mean being predictable in the sense of having hash and beans for breakfast every day. In this context consistency is drawing a straight line between your values and your actions—and making sure everyone else can see it.

A friend of mine took his family to live in Charlotte, North Carolina, where they'd bought a home. The people next door immediately visited them, talked about the gospel, and invited them to church. Tom explained that he was already a Christian and an active member of a congregation. They took no notice. "Come to our church," they insisted, "where they really preach the gospel."

An empty lot owned by those neighbors separated the homes. Tom had two sons who liked to play baseball, and they started using the lot as a ballpark. His sons invited their friends to play with them—most of them non-Christians. As a result, three of the boys started attending Sunday school regularly.

This ought to have pleased the neighbors, but it didn't. They chased the boys off the lot and soon planted two maple trees in strategic spots so that no one could use the area for games. Other incidents like this had occurred earlier. It seemed as though Tom's neighbors showed a blatant disregard for other people's interests. Yet during this time the neighbors still visited Tom regularly. Each time they came with one purpose—to invite him to "our church, where the pastor really knows how to get people saved."

There may be more to this situation than meets the eye. Just because Tom's neighbors chased the kids off the lot doesn't mean they were mean-spirited spoilsports. They might have disliked the noise, thought the kids would ruin their grass, or worried that somebody would get hurt on their property and they'd be legally responsible. But that wasn't the *impression* they gave. To Tom and his family, the neighbors' Christian commitment appeared to extend no further than witnessing about Jesus Christ and inviting people to "our church, where they really preach the gospel." Consequently, and without being judgmental, Tom saw a chasm "between what they profess and what they possess." If there was a straight line between these people's values and their behavior, it wasn't obvious.

Many years ago I heard a preacher quote an unbeliever's assertion that if Jesus came back to earth today "He wouldn't become a Christian." The rest of the sermon is lost to my memory, but that statement penetrated deeply. He was saying, I think, that many people who profess to love Jesus Christ actually live unchristian lives. Yet the call to straighten out the line between Christian values and behavior isn't one we can neglect.

> *No one can lay any foundation other than the one already laid, which is Jesus Christ. If any man builds on this foundation using gold, silver, costly stones, wood, hay or straw, his work will be shown for what it is, because the Day will bring it to light. It will be revealed with fire, and the fire will test the quality of each man's work. If what he has built survives, he will receive his reward. If it is burned up, he will suffer loss; he himself will be saved, but only as one escaping through the flames. (1 Corinthians 3:11–15)*

It's worth remembering that Paul endured far more provocation in his lifetime than any of us. He was imprisoned, maligned, stoned, hounded, shipwrecked. Yet in every situation he found the resources to give thanks to God and to be—if not exactly "happy" in the way we mean it today—deeply joyful and contented. In every adverse circumstance, he showed what he believed by the way he reacted to his circumstances.

Note again how Paul stresses *personal* responsibility for decision making. If our conversion is the work of an Agency outside ourselves, what happens afterward is unquestionably under our own control. We choose the materials with which to build our lives. Those materials can be strong or weak, more or less able to withstand the testing fires. The mark of our maturity in Christ isn't what others see in us now but what will endure to eternity.

When Jesus is in the executive suite, our short-term profits matter less than our long-term contribution to God's corporation. It's not necessarily today's high-fliers whose names will appear tomorrow on the company's roll of honor, and there is a spillover from that into our working lives. When people see consistency, they see a character they can trust. If there's one thing worse than having a religious person in the office, it's having a religious person in the office who doesn't live up to his own beliefs. Aim to be admirable.

6

AGGRESSIVENESS:
Beyond Intimidation

Television interviews fascinate me. I don't gain much information about the persons being interviewed, but I *do* learn about the interviewer.

Barbara Walters, one of ABC's most popular interviewers, has a reputation for tenacity and aggression, so much so that someone has said, "You can almost see her fangs." In the political arena particularly, critics have accused her of being thoughtless and rude. Yet with people she obviously admires she comes across very differently. She can seem awestruck, even fawning.

In this respect, Walters is just like many others in her profession. She's also like many of us. We quake before important people and cower before celebrities. Logically, we know that these individuals are just ordinary folks: they catch colds and have laundry to wash. But we don't treat them that way. Perhaps it's because of their wealth, their fame, or their glittering smiles; or maybe it's because deference to the rich and famous is as old as time itself. Whatever the reason, we look up to some people and down on others.

Looking up to another person makes us feel threatened and intimidated. It's what Joseph's brothers felt when they confronted him as virtual ruler of Egypt: "Please, my lord," said Judah, "let your servant speak a word to my lord. Do not be angry with your servant, though you are equal to Pharaoh himself" (Genesis 44:18). To be intimidated is to feel that another person has power over you, just as Joseph had power over his brothers. It's an experience all too common in the management hierarchies of the corporate world. Intimidation could be your boss's middle name. And people tend to react to that in one of two ways: either they grovel and try to avoid the other person, or they dig in their heels and become rude and abusive.

But if Jesus is in the executive suite, intimidation goes out the window. Look at two biblical examples of people who had to cross status gaps to deal with people: Paul and Nehemiah.

STAY COOL

The most casual reading of the New Testament reveals that nobody intimidated Paul. No one made him afraid. No one unnerved or menaced him—a remarkable fact, given that he'd been beaten up, stoned, and almost killed on several occasions. His friends, in fact, were far more concerned for Paul's well-being than Paul was.

When, near the end of his ministry, he chose to set out for Jerusalem, many of his loving friends and coworkers tried to discourage him. Agabus, a prophet, warned him of the trials he would face. But Paul stood as firmly then as he'd done at any other time: "'Why are you weeping and breaking my heart? I am ready not only to be bound, but also to die in Jerusalem for the name of the Lord Jesus.' When he would not be dissuaded, we gave up and said, 'The Lord's will be done'" (Acts 21:13–14).

Paul had long passed the point where his own safety rated more than secondary consideration. He knew what God wanted him to do, and he refused to let anything deter him. He went on to Jerusalem.

Soon after he arrived there the Jews caused a riot. They started beating him, and he was saved only by the intervention of Roman soldiers. While the soldiers placed him under arrest, the crowd, who wanted Paul dead, screamed, "Away with him!"

Amazingly, though, as the guards led him to their barracks, Paul asked the commander for permission to speak to the crowd. A lesser man would have cut and run and been thankful to get protection. But not Paul. Fully aware that a few moments earlier this crowd had been ready to tear him limb from limb, he nevertheless sought another opportunity to speak. From the stairway of the barracks he began to address them in Aramaic, and—surprisingly—"they became very quiet" (Acts 22:2).

Paul told the crowd about his background, repeated the story of the Damascus road, and then went on to testify that Jesus was God's Christ. When he repeated the Lord's command to him, "Go; I will send you far away to the Gentiles" (22:21), the crowed once again turned nasty. He escaped with his life only because the guards dragged him up into the barracks. So began a phase of Paul's career during which, between long stays in prison, he confronted the region's top political leaders.

When the Roman commander Claudius Lysias learned of a plot to kill Paul, Claudius dispatched him to Caesarea to appear before Governor Felix: "Felix . . . sent for Paul and listened to him as he spoke about faith in Christ Jesus. As Paul discoursed on righteousness, self-control and the judgment to come, Felix was afraid and said, 'That's enough for now! You may leave. When I find it convenient, I will send for you'" (Acts 24:24–25). Paul talked, and Felix became afraid—hardly the expected outcome of a meeting between a prisoner and a political leader. For two years Paul languished in prison because Felix refused to upset the Jews by releasing him.

Then Felix was succeeded as Judean procurator by Porcius Festus. We do not have a record of Paul's testimony before the new governor, but we do have a record of his testimony before King Agrippa. When Agrippa visited Caesarea, Festus told him about the now-famous prisoner, and Agrippa agreed to hear Paul.

Agrippa, the last of the Herods, had been born in the luxury of Rome and had returned with the emperor's favor as ruler of the Jewish people. He was powerful and well connected. Nevertheless, Paul treated him as he had Felix and Festus. He again boldly gave a defense of his faith in Christ:

> *Agrippa said to Paul, "You have permission to speak for yourself."*
>
> *So Paul motioned with his hand and began his defense: "King Agrippa, I consider myself fortunate to stand before you today as I make my defense against all the accusations of the Jews, and especially so because you are well acquainted with all the Jewish customs and controversies. Therefore, I beg you to listen to me patiently. (Acts 26:1–3)*

When Paul spoke to King Agrippa, he approached a man who understood the Jewish faith, a man of intellectual acumen and worldly desires. He launched into his testimony of salvation (which Luke also records in Acts 9 and 22). He told of his commission as a Jewish zealot to wipe out the Christian faith, then of his conversion. But, as usual, his defense rested not only on his personal experience but on the basics of faith in Jesus Christ—especially on the Resurrection, which still distinguishes Christianity from Judaism.

Paul did faithfully what God had called him to do.

It was at the mention of the Resurrection that Festus interrupted. Perhaps he felt uncomfortable with Paul's straightforward manner in addressing the king and with Paul's assertion that "the Christ would suffer and, as the first to rise from the dead, would proclaim light to his own people and to the Gentiles" (Acts 26:23).

"You are out of your mind, Paul!" Festus shouted. "Your great learning is driving you insane" (verse 24).

Paul, however, calmly replied, "I am not insane, most excellent Festus. What I am saying is true and reasonable. The king is familiar with these things, and I can speak freely to him. I am convinced that none of this has escaped his notice, because it was not done in a corner" (verses 25–26).

With that, he returned his attention to Agrippa: "'King Agrippa, do you believe the prophets? I know you do.' Then Agrippa said to Paul, 'Do you think that in such a short time you can persuade me to be a Christian?'" (verses 27–28).

Paul knew exactly what he was aiming for: "Short time or long—I pray God that not only you but all who are listening to me today may become what I am, except for these chains" (verse 29).

The king rose, and because he rose everyone else had to rise as well. Then they all left the room (verses 30–31). We have no evidence that Agrippa ever turned to Jesus Christ. Yet regardless of the outcome, Paul did faithfully what God had called him to do. And he was so persuasive that Agrippa privately conceded that if Paul hadn't appealed to Caesar he could have been set free (verse 32).

The king, who no doubt was accustomed to having people flatter and fear him, found in Paul an intellectual equal. Paul believed that the civil authorities were placed there by divine intention. So he did not antagonize Agrippa by disregarding his privileges as king—although his hope that "all who are listening to me today may become what I am" makes few concessions to status. On the other hand, he did not act like a servant. His manner was polite but firm—just as it would have been with anyone.

PLAYING THE ORGANIZATION

Nehemiah was an organization man. He was also a man close to the centers of power. Being cupbearer to King Artaxerxes did not make him an equal, but it gave him the opportunity to communicate with the king—if the king so chose. When Nehemiah received the bad news from Jerusalem, he could have abused his position and brought his request to the king outright. He didn't, knowing that to do so would probably have cost him his head. The king had to make the first move. Nehemiah had learned the protocol, and he observed it:

I took the wine and gave it to the king. I had not been sad in his presence before; so the king asked me, "Why does your face look so sad when you are not ill? This can be nothing but sadness of heart."

I was very much afraid, but I said to the king, "May the king live forever! Why should my face not look sad when the city where my fathers are buried lies in ruins, and its gates have been destroyed by fire?"

The king said to me, "What is it you want?" (Nehemiah 2:1–4)

That Nehemiah was afraid is understandable: unlike Paul, he'd had little practice in speaking before the powerful. But he did not allow his feelings to infect his actions. When asked to explain himself, he did so plainly. He didn't apologize for looking glum, nor did he shrink from specifics. Artaxerxes asked for Nehemiah's business plan, and Nehemiah delivered it:

"If it pleases the king and if your servant has found favor in his sight, let him send me to the city in Judah where my fathers are buried so that I can rebuild it."

Then the king, with the queen sitting beside him, asked me, "How long will your journey take, and when will you get back?" It pleased the king to send me; so I set a time.

I also said to him, "If it pleases the king, may I have letters to the governors of Trans-Euphrates, so that they will provide me safe-conduct until I arrive in Judah? And may I have a letter to Asaph, keeper of the king's forest, so he will give me timber to make beams for the gates of the citadel by the temple and for the city wall and for the residence I will occupy?" (Nehemiah 2:5–8)

Like Paul, Nehemiah had prepared thoroughly. He knew exactly what he wanted to say, and this contributed to his confidence. He did not respond with "I need time to think about that." He had all the necessary information at his fingertips. Preparation, however, does not explain the refusal of either Paul or Nehemiah to be intimidated in the presence of a king. As Nehemiah tells us, "because the gracious hand of my God was upon me, the king granted my requests" (verse 8).

This should not be taken to mean that God pulled the wool over Artaxerxes' eyes so that he said yes to something he'd usually have said no to. God's gracious hand was on Nehemiah in the sense that Nehemiah took proper account of God in his dealings with the king. The fact that he dared make his request and that he took the considerable risk of looking downcast in the king's presence shows that Nehemiah recognized God's supremacy. The line of command did not stop with Artaxerxes, and Nehemiah knew it. It stopped with God. What God approved, the king was helpless to oppose.

It was the same with Paul. Standing in the presence of a king made little difference to the apostle; he had ended up in prison because he served the King of kings. It was a matter of little account, then, that the King of kings should require him to address Agrippa. In the corporation Paul worked for, Agrippa was a middle manager. Jesus occupied the executive suite.

TWO CURES FOR INTIMIDATION

You may feel that Paul and Nehemiah are a long way from your own situation. That's true. An English vicar is supposed to have remarked once, "When Paul visited a city he stirred up a riot. When I visit, they serve me tea." At the same time, their example provides enduring lessons for us.

1. Care About the People Above You

Paul cared. It's that simple. No matter how forcefully he spoke, the reader still gets a strong sense of his caring heart. He felt pain over their rejection of God, and he was willing to go to almost any lengths to help them give their lives to God.

By contrast, much of our conduct in the workplace is characterized by clumsiness and unconcern. Nowhere is this more true than in the area of witnessing. Several years ago, two friends of mine had been talking with a businessman regularly about Jesus Christ. One day he invited them to go to a spa with him. After their workout they entered the steam room, and one of them was getting ready to start talking about the Lord when another man walked in and sat down nearby.

He nodded to them and said, "Sure is hot in here, isn't it?"

"Yes," one of them answered, assuming that he was trying to make conversation.

"Yeah," the man repeated, "sure is hot." Then he added, "But not half as hot as hell is going to be for the sinners who reject Jesus Christ."

The remark fell like a brick. Not surprisingly, the non-Christian got up and walked out, shaking his head. After that he never allowed the conversation to stray onto God or anything else to do with the faith.

I'm not telling this story to condemn the man's zeal. The point is that he spoke zealously but without sensitivity. He didn't pause to think who the three strangers were, what their needs might be, even whether they wanted to engage in conversation. He demonstrated no real concern for them. They were just targets for evangelism.

No doubt, if you asked him, he would profess to care for the whole human race and claim that his bullheaded witnessing expressed this care. But caring for the human race in general and caring for specific individuals are not the same thing. I don't believe we can be concerned about others unless we know something about them. Concern grows out of a context and flows from a relationship. If I don't relate to you as another human being, how can I possibly care about your needs and your relationship to God?

As I think again of Paul, this was the essence of his unique compassion. When he spoke to crowds, he preached theological truths. But when he spoke to individuals—like Agrippa—he treated them as people with unique characteristics and concerns. He knew Agrippa's background. And that's what made his interaction with the king so effective. He didn't go with a prepared formula or a string of memorized verses that might or might not fit the need of the moment. He knew who he was talking to—he knew the person, not just the office that person held.

*If the boss's instructions and your moral code part
company, your commitment lies with the latter.*

Care, then, is a central element of a Christian's approach
to relationships in the business world. Care ensures that we
see another person's humanity, even when he or she is being
overbearing or unreasonable. It keeps us from being angry
and resentful and preserves an all-important focus on the
job being done. The boss may tell us, "Get that report on my
desk by five o'clock," or may say, "I'd really appreciate getting that report this afternoon, if you can manage it." Either
way, care requires us to complete and deliver it on time with
a polite smile.

2. Trust God to Back You Up

Paul trusted. Nehemiah trusted. They both honestly
believed that God was with them and that God would give
them whatever support they required in their pursuit of His
work. Knowing they had the backing of the person at the
top lent an edge to their dealings with the wealthy and powerful. Without having laid eyes on Jesus, they had internal-
ized the truth Jesus Himself told Pilate: "You would have no
power over me if it were not given to you from above" (John
19:11).

Consider Paul's appearing before the two governors and
King Agrippa. Not impressed by his surroundings, not intimidated by royalty, Paul simply defended his faith. Although a
prisoner, he was God's prisoner. He respected the ruler, but
his loyalty went to a higher power. In other words, your boss
at work is not the ultimate authority. If the boss's instructions and your moral code part company, your commitment
lies with the latter. Care requires us to be charitable to a
superior who adopts an intimidating manner; trust assures
us that there are limits beyond which intimidation should
not be tolerated and actions to which we should not assent,
whether we are intimidated or bribed.

In the end, we cannot attain the boldness exemplified in

the lives of Nehemiah and Paul unless we first surrender to someone greater than ourselves. That someone is Jesus Christ. Our confidence comes via our obedience: if we keep faith as employees in God's corporation, no one can touch us. But our relationship with Jesus doesn't only keep us from being intimidated; it also forbids us to intimidate.

AS I HAVE LOVED YOU . . .

When Peter asked Jesus how many times one person should forgive another, Jesus told him a story. There was a servant who owed his master a massive amount of money—millions of dollars, in today's currency. So the master had decided to sell the man and his family in an effort to recoup the debt. But upon hearing the servant's pleas, he changed his mind. Instead, in a show of unprecedented largesse, the master canceled the man's debt and let him go.

But the story doesn't end there. After the servant left his master's house, he came across one of his colleagues, a man who owed him "a hundred denarii"—in other words, just a few dollars. Did he embrace the man and tell him his debt was forgiven? No way:

> He grabbed him and began to choke him. "Pay back what you owe me!" he demanded.
>
> His fellow servant fell to his knees and begged him, "Be patient with me, and I will pay you back."
>
> But he refused. Instead, he went off and had the man thrown into prison until he could pay the debt. When the other servants saw what had happened, they were greatly distressed and went and told their master everything that had happened.
>
> Then the master called the servant in. "You wicked servant," he said, "I canceled all that debt of yours because you begged me to. Shouldn't you have had mercy on your fellow servant just as I had on you?" In anger his master turned him over to the jailers to be tortured, until he should pay back all he owed. (Matthew 18:28–34)

It is as harsh a warning against bullying as you could hope to find. That someone owes you makes no difference. Each of us has been forgiven immeasurably more than we could be owed by another. We are all forgiven; therefore, we must all forgive.

But there is more to the parable than this. The ungrateful servant treated his debtor exactly as he'd begged his master *not* to treat him. This parallel does more than excite our sense of injustice. A psychiatrist might argue that the servant's behavior reflected a negative self-image; in other words, he felt incompetent for having let himself get into debt and compensated for this by intimidating his own debtor.

This kind of mental process is remarkably common. A person who sees imperfections in others' work will often be acutely conscious of imperfections in his own. Intimidating his friends and colleagues allows him to transfer the guilt of failure to another person. It's the old story of the school bully who's unpleasant not because he's bad but because he's unhappy. The intimidator feels intimidated.

If we have the urge to be short-tempered or aggressive with others, we should ask whether the anger we feel is directed toward the other person or toward ourselves. In many cases, I suspect, we will find that we are getting mad at somebody so as to hide our own frustration.

The strongest contrast to the ungrateful servant in the Gospels is the chief tax collector Zacchaeus, a diminutive and deeply unpopular man who had to climb a tree in order to catch a glimpse of Jesus in the crowd:

> When Jesus reached the spot, he looked up and said to him, "Zacchaeus, come down immediately. I must stay at your house today." So he came down at once and welcomed him gladly.
>
> All the people saw this and began to mutter, "He has gone to be the guest of a 'sinner.'"
>
> But Zacchaeus stood up and said to the Lord, "Look, Lord! Here and now I give half of my possessions to the poor, and if I have cheated anybody out of anything, I will pay back four times the amount."

Jesus said to him, "Today salvation has come to this house."
(Luke 19:5–9)

Zacchaeus was probably one of the most intimidating people in Jerusalem: a collector of taxes (never a popular profession) and, worse, by virtue of his job, a collaborator with the Roman authorities. All this and more Jesus forgave Zacchaeus the instant He called him down from the tree. And if Zacchaeus had been like the ungrateful servant of the parable, he would have gone right back to his tax office the next day to continue defrauding his fellow Jews. But Zacchaeus—perhaps owing to his unpopularity—understood forgiveness and valued it above all else. He didn't need to intimidate. In Jesus he had all the security and assurance he needed—qualities money had been unable to give him. Forgiven, he could now forgive. In God's corporation, the corporate policy can be summed up in those famous words, "Go thou, and do likewise."

7

SELF-KNOWLEDGE:
Who Are You?

In February 1984 the executive board of a major international missions organization voted me president. At that time I already worked as managing director. But the offer was a heady thing for a thirty-six-year-old, not least because the invitation came with the backing of the founder. I prayed about it and thought about it for a long time—and then turned it down.

Turning down any kind of job with the title "president" attached to it is a tough proposition. As a friend of mine has remarked, in the normal run of things the only way you get to call yourself president of an organization is to start it yourself—then you can be president right away! But to be *voted* president—that's different. Almost always a president gets more money, more power, heaps more prestige. And even if he gets none of those things, the mere title would make him walk taller and put a new spring in his step. Getting to be president is no mean achievement. Why on earth did I turn down the chance?

For a long time I had enjoyed the confidence and trust of the organization's founder and executive board. I felt that I functioned optimally in my position as managing director, which meant that the organization had little to gain by promoting me. And as for status, it really didn't bother me whether people called me "managing director" or "president," since my identity relied on neither.

I believe that identity is one of the most important issues facing those in leadership—whether as parents, executives, or ministers. It decides how you define who you are and what gives you your significance as a person.

We make some typical and costly mistakes in this area. Parents have the responsibility of raising their children to be healthy adults. Yet parents often define "who they are" by the kind of neighborhood they live in, how many cars they own, how many prestigious clubs they belong to, or how many high-tech gadgets they have lying around the house. Not surprisingly, the children follow suit. "Who they are" depends on how many toys they have and how much the toys cost.

In this situation, identity keeps on changing. Who you are as a rising junior manager in your twenties has little to do with who you are as a company executive in your fifties. Not only are you older, your identity, defined in terms of status symbols, has completely changed. Once you were struggling; now you've made it.

But what happens if your financial fortunes take a turn for the worse? You're forced to move into a smaller house, maybe go bankrupt. You lose all those symbols by which you defined yourself. Not only that, but you probably lose the friends whose admiration depended on the things you owned.

DOWN WITH THE PIGS

Jesus' story of the prodigal son (see Luke 15:11–32) is very much about the identity of the down-and-outer. When the farmer's younger son demands, "Father, give me my share of the estate" (verse 12), he is cashing in his family identity. He does not wish to be known as the son and joint-heir of a wealthy landowner. Instead, he sets off for a "distant country," where his identity is expressed solely in terms of his wealth. He gathers around him a group of so-called friends who see him not as the person he is in his family and community but as a wealthy young man who throws wild parties. Then comes the fall:

SELF-KNOWLEDGE: *Who Are You?*

After he had spent everything, there was a severe famine in that whole country, and he began to be in need. So he went and hired himself out to a citizen of that country, who sent him to his fields to feed pigs. He longed to fill his stomach with the pods that the pigs were eating, but no one gave him anything.

When he came to his senses, he said, "How many of my father's hired men have food to spare, and here I am starving to death! I will set out and go back to my father and say to him: Father, I have sinned against heaven and against you. I am no longer worthy to be called your son; make me like one of your hired men." (verses 14–19)

None of the friends he gained in his wealthy days stuck around to help him when he went into the red. He'd vested his whole identity in his cash, and when his money ran out his identity evaporated; in a sense, he no longer existed. Not surprisingly, it occurs to him that—since he's defined himself in terms of money—he'd be better off as his father's employee than as a swineherd. We know what happened next:

But while he was still a long way off, his father saw him and was filled with compassion for him; he ran to his son, threw his arms around him and kissed him. . . .

The father said to his servants, "Quick! Bring the best robe and put it on him. Put a ring on his finger and sandals on his feet. Bring the fattened calf and kill it. Let's have a feast and celebrate. For this son of mine was dead and is alive again; he was lost and is found." (verses 20, 22–24)

> *Leaders in business who motivate their employees only by financial rewards are, in effect, asking those people to see themselves in financial terms.*

This is more than the exuberance of an anxious and bereft father. The father bestows on his son the identity the son had cast aside. That the son has returned penniless, having squandered half the family estate, means nothing in comparison to the fact that he has, in a sense, returned from the dead. At home he *is* his father's son. He could not be received as an employee. He was lost—and now he is found.

KNOW WHO YOU ARE

One interpretation of Jesus' story highlights the difference between permanent and transient identities. The problem is particularly acute in business. Leaders in business who motivate their employees only by *financial* rewards are, in effect, asking those people to see themselves in financial terms. The result is that everyone feels good until the recession hits. Then the pay-freezes and the lay-offs begin, and the people who felt they were "something" financially start to have doubts. Demoralization and alienation set in. Everyone fights to win a bigger piece of the shrinking pie. And why not? The employer has taught them to build their identity on their paychecks. Now he reaps the rewards.

Today, the successful companies are those who have managed to reach down to the workers and involve them in the decision-making process. They have built their employees' identity not on the paycheck but on the company and the values it stands for. Consequently, when a crisis hits, the employees remain confident that their opinions will be heard and continue to feel motivated. They are "part of the team" first and wage earners second. If the wages don't rise, they're still on the team, still playing to win. They have a permanent identity in the company, not a transient one.

But, of course, the parable of the prodigal son says far more than this. The father stands for God, and the rebellious son for sinful humankind. In other words, when we come to Christ, we discover—or perhaps rediscover—our true identity as God's children. That is what we are before all else. And that is what we remain. If we lose everything else in life—our money, our status, our occupation, our family, our friends, our health—we will still be welcomed home as God's children. The best robe will be brought out for us, the ring put on our finger.

Inwardly, as Christians, we realize this. God has given us an instinctive need to belong, and in belonging at the deepest level—to whatever—we receive a satisfaction and fulfillment far greater than we could achieve by the accumulation of wealth. Indeed, the drive to accumulate wealth is often a way in which a person tries to compensate for his or her lack of a genuine, permanent identity.

CONTROL YOUR ROLES

Parents need to get their identities in the right order. Throughout life we take on numerous transient identities based on the roles we perform. But whereas these transient identities can be very important, we should never use them as our deepest reasons for living, nor should we encourage our children to do so—for two reasons.

First, only one identity lasts forever. If I'm a bank president, I'll remain a bank president only until I retire or change jobs or die. If I'm a father, I remain a father until I die. But if I'm a Christian, I remain a Christian for eternity. By all means we should take pride in our work, and we should rejoice to be members of a particular family or a particular congregation. But far more important than my membership in a company or a family or a church is that I belong to God's corporation. I have accepted the call of a lifetime. That alone will outlast the world I live in. That alone cannot be taken away.

Second, transient identities or roles are fickle. A child wholly absorbed in the quest to become a football player may never achieve that goal. Furthermore, once achieved, it doesn't last. Even world-class sportsmen and sportswomen can usually maintain peak physical fitness only until their mid-thirties: age takes away strength just as it takes away beauty. Long before the passage of time forces the football player to retire, a run of injuries or bad luck may get him dropped from the team. Roles, in other words, are time-bound and dependent on our ability to fulfill them. Wait a while, or fail to make the grade, and the role disappears, taking the identity with it.

From a very early age, children should be taught that they are a gift from God. They were known to God before they were born and live in this world by divine appointment. God knows them by name and loves them so much that He gave them a special function and calling. No matter what happens in life, no one can ever take that away from them.

BE WHO YOU ARE

While traveling in southern Europe, it is said, the great French artist Gustave Doré once lost his passport. When he came to the Spanish border and the guards asked him for identification, he said, "I have lost my papers. But you can trust me, I am Gustave Doré, the artist. Please let me proceed."

"Oh, no," said the border guards. "Many travelers represent themselves as important people. How do we know you are who you claim to be?"

A lengthy discussion ensued, which was solved only when the commanding officer intervened. "Here is a pencil and paper," he said. "If you are a famous artist, prove it by drawing a picture."

With masterful hand, Doré quickly sketched some of the features of the surrounding landscape. He showed the sketch to the officer, who immediately nodded.

"Now I am perfectly sure of who you are," he exclaimed. "Only Gustave Doré could do that."

The point, of course, is that Doré needed to demonstrate his identity for others to see it. *He* knew who he was, but the border guards could share his knowledge only when he expressed his identity in action. Identity that leaves no impression on the personality is of dubious value. We are not only asked to *be* Christians but to *act* like Christians. In God's corporation we have a job to do.

At the same time, Gustave Doré did not spend his whole time drawing pictures and handing them around, saying,

"Hey, here's a picture. This proves I'm Gustave Doré."
Though his identity was expressed regularly in his work,
that wasn't his reason for working. He used his work to
prove his identity only when the occasion demanded it.

That is important to remember when we look at the life
and ministry of Jesus. It is remarkable, for instance, how
seldom Jesus allowed the news of His miracles to be publi-
cized. Look at the story of Jairus, a ruler of the synagogue,
who implored Jesus to come and heal his only daughter:

> *When he arrived at the house of Jairus, he did not let anyone
> go in with him except Peter, John and James, and the child's father
> and mother. Meanwhile, all the people were wailing and mourn-
> ing for her. "Stop wailing," Jesus said. "She is not dead but asleep."*
>
> *They laughed at him, knowing that she was dead. But he took
> her by the hand and said, "My child, get up!" Her spirit returned,
> and at once she stood up. Then Jesus told them to give her some-
> thing to eat. Her parents were astonished, but he ordered them not
> to tell anyone what had happened. (Luke 8:51–56)*

Think of the fund-raising opportunities a story like that
would bring. And yet what did Jesus do? "He ordered them
not to tell anyone what had happened." No doubt Jesus had
His own strategic reasons for avoiding sensational publici-
ty. But, more important, He felt no need to push Himself
forward. It was in His nature to do the miraculous; He had
compassion on the sick and the suffering, and because He
was God He healed their infirmities. But He never per-
formed a miracle with the aim of drawing attention to Himself.

Why would He need to? After all, He was the one for
whom and through whom the entire universe was creat-
ed—every last galaxy and planet and star. Being incarnated
as a man did not dilute His divine identity. Voluntarily
stripping Himself of His divine glory did not shake His confidence. And because He knew who He was, it didn't matter
to Him whether people liked Him or approved of Him. The
only approval He sought was His Father's.

To be sure, Jesus wanted others to believe His message

and follow Him—after all, others would have to carry His message after the Ascension. But His certainty about His own identity allowed Him to do miracles not for His own sake—to affirm who He was—but for the sake of those He had come to serve. This certainty steeled Him against the kind of adversity under which lesser men would have crumpled. Accusations that He was illegitimate, that His power came from the Devil, that His claim to forgive sins made Him a blaspheming upstart—none of these things fazed Him.

Jesus knew where He had come from, what He was doing, and where He was going. His identity wasn't up for grabs. It wasn't open to be molded by public opinion or fine-tuned by marketing strategists. On the contrary, it was defined solely in terms of His divine origin and His divine mission. One succinct summary of it, in fact, can be found in the "I am" sayings in the gospel of John:

"I am the bread of life" to the unsatisfied (6:35).
"I am the light of the world" for the blind (9:5).
"I am the gate" of salvation for the unsaved (10:7).
"I am the good shepherd" for the lost (10:11).
"I am the resurrection and the life" for the dead (11:25).
"I am the way" for the ignorant (14:6).
"I am the true vine" for the fruitless (15:1).

Consequently, Jesus never took any account of the status of those to whom He spoke. Nicodemus, who came to talk to Jesus in secret, was a member of the highest ruling council in Israel. Yet Jesus expresses a polite but firm surprise at the man's ignorance: "You are Israel's teacher," said Jesus, "and do you not understand these things? I tell you the truth, we speak of what we know, and we testify to what we have seen, but still you people do not accept our testimony" (John 3:10–11).

A little later He breaks with convention by addressing a Samaritan woman:

> *When a Samaritan woman came to draw water, Jesus said to her, "Will you give me a drink?" (His disciples had gone into the town to buy food.)*
>
> *The Samaritan woman said to him, "You are a Jew and I am a Samaritan woman. How can you ask me for a drink?" (For Jews do not associate with Samaritans.)*
>
> *Jesus answered her, "If you knew the gift of God and who it is that asks you for a drink, you would have asked him and he would have given you living water." (John 4:7–10)*

Presented with the president or the pope, you would find it hard not to show some degree of deference. But presented with a woman who is virtually a prostitute, you'd find it hard not to look down on her—either as a moral reprobate or as a victim of circumstance. Yet Jesus adopted the same tone with both Nicodemus and the Samaritan woman. The encounters did not impact His identity or change His demeanor or affect His attitude—simply because He knew who He was.

How different from the average modern man or woman. More often our identities are like barometers, reflecting whatever conditions we happen to find ourselves in. We are, in Paul's phrase, "all things to all men," not out of a deliberate attempt to find common ground but because we are so unsure of what God really wants us to be. Yet being who we are should be so simple.

WHAT MATTERS IS THE GROUND YOU STAND ON

People often ask me how I feel, as an Egyptian by birth, pastoring a fast-growing Anglican church in the southern states of America. This question mostly comes from northerners. Notice the assumptions it makes about identity. I "am" first and foremost an "Egyptian." The most important thing about me, in other words, is my ethnic origin—one that renders me a displaced person anywhere but in the country where I was born.

*My identity does not come from my degrees or from
my achievements or from my ethnic background.*

You will have had many similar questions asked of you.
For instance, what does it feel like to be a woman executive
working on a predominantly male board? How does it feel
to be a mature student going back to school? How does it
feel to be black in a white neighborhood, or white in a black
neighborhood? And so on.

In my own case, the honest answer is that I've never
given these feelings a second thought. Nor have the members of my lay leadership team, most of whom are my close
friends. God, who has called me to this work, is the one
from whom and in whom I find my identity. My identity
does not come from my degrees or from my achievements
or from my ethnic background. It does not even come from
God's favor in the growth of the church. It comes solely
from the promises written in His Word. What God says
about me makes all the difference.

The French emperor Napoleon was reviewing his troops
one day when his horse reared, out of control. The great
man was in danger of being hurled to the ground until a
young private leaped from the ranks, grabbed the horse's
bridle, and subdued it.

"Thank you, Captain," said Napoleon—thus bestowing
upon the private an instant promotion.

Smiling proudly, the soldier inquired, "Of what regi-
ment, sir?"

"Of my guard," called Napoleon as he dashed away
down the lines.

Immediately assuming his new rank, the private-
turned-captain walked over to join a group of staff officers.

"What is this insolent fellow doing here?" one of them
asked. They all looked at him.

"I am a captain of the guard," the young man replied.

"You rascal," the officer said. "You are just a private.
What makes you think you are a captain?"

The young man pointed to the departing emperor and confidently responded, "He said it!"

"Then I beg your pardon, Captain," the officer answered politely. "I was not aware of your promotion."

The young soldier did not feel like a captain, nor had he been issued a captain's insignia. All he had was the word of his leader, Napoleon. But that was enough.

As Christians we are in a remarkably similar position. In God's corporation we do not receive paychecks or have job descriptions. These formal signs of our membership are largely absent. Instead, we have the cast-iron assurance of the Bible:

> *Therefore, if anyone is in Christ, he is a new creation; the old has gone, the new has come! All this is from God, who reconciled us to himself through Christ and gave us the ministry of reconciliation: that God was reconciling the world to himself in Christ, not counting men's sins against them. And he has committed to us the message of reconciliation. We are therefore Christ's ambassadors.* (2 Corinthians 5:17–20)

Christians, Paul goes on to say, are "God's fellow workers" (2 Corinthians 6:1). And, of course, that remains true, whatever happens to our other roles and relationships. It is the deepest identity we have. And because it is the deepest and is bestowed on us by the Word of God, it is the basis both of our psychological security and of our firm attachment to principle.

The celebrated Scottish athlete Eric Liddell could have seen himself as a sportsman first and a Christian second. When he went to Paris for the 1924 Olympics, it was in his roles as a champion sprinter and a representative of Great Britain. Yet when the crunch came—when he realized that the heat for his event was going to be held on a Sunday—it was his Christian identity that won out. Despite his desperate desire to win the gold medal, and despite the strongest possible pressure from his team's authorities, he refused to run on the Sabbath. Like Jesus, he knew who he was. And that's why we remember him.

8

FAILURE:
One Mistake and You're Out!

I t stands at a prestigious location—Wall Street, Manhattan. It has a marble frontage, with angels and trumpets in relief on the door lintels and gleaming brass handrails the to right and left of the steps. As you approach, a uniformed doorman opens the heavy translucent doors (scenes of heaven etched on the glass), letting you pass into a red-carpeted vestibule, where each of the twelve elevators is lined with a different precious stone. A solid gold plaque suspended from the ceiling tells you you're at the head offices of God Incorporated. . . .

Ridiculous? Of course. God doesn't occupy the top floor of an office tower, nor does He relate to us literally as though we were employees in His company. When I talk about Jesus in the executive suite, I am using the corporation not as a *description* of the church but as a *metaphor* to give extra impact to our understanding of the call of a lifetime. Yet at the time Jesus actually walked and talked with His disciples, the similarities to a corporation were particularly striking. In organizational terms, Jesus was the Chairman. He had an executive committee made up of three members: Peter as CEO, James as COO, and John as vice president of public relations. And, of course, in the twelve apostles He had a full board of directors.

Anyone who has been on a corporate board will know that no two members are alike. For one thing, each has his or her own temperament and idiosyncrasies. Not only that but, despite sharing the leadership of the same corporation, they usually have very different ideas about the way that corporation should be run. They have their own private agendas—and those private agendas not infrequently conflict with that of the chairman.

JESUS IN THE BOARDROOM

All this can be shown to have been true of the twelve disciples.

> *People were also bringing babies to Jesus to have him touch them. When the disciples saw this, they rebuked them. But Jesus called the children to him and said, "Let the little children come to me, and do not hinder them, for the kingdom of God belongs to such as these." (Luke 18:15–16)*

Clearly, the disciples had a misguided notion of what it means to be important. "Important people," in their book, didn't stop to cuddle strangers' babies. In the serious, adult world of religious leadership, children had no place. Mistaking importance for self-importance (a common error in corporate boardrooms!), they naturally competed among themselves for whatever honors they supposed to be in the offing. That's why, on the road to Capernaum, we find the disciples engaged in a muffled, and thoroughly childish, dispute about which of them was the "greatest."

That the kingdom of God belonged to the childlike rather than to the childish was a lesson it took the disciples a long time to absorb. The same misunderstanding lay behind a dispute between the Chairman and the rest of the "board":

> *Then James and John, the sons of Zebedee, came to him. "Teacher," they said, "we want you to do for us whatever we ask."*
> *"What do you want me to do for you?" he asked.*
> *They replied, "Let one of us sit at your right and the other at your left in your glory." . . .*

When the ten heard about this, they became indignant with James and John. Jesus called them together and said, "You know that those who are regarded as rulers of the Gentiles lord it over them, and their high officials exercise authority over them. Not so with you. Instead, whoever wants to become great among you must be your servant, and whoever wants to be first must be slave of all. For even the Son of Man did not come to be served, but to serve, and to give his life as a ransom for many." (Mark 10:35–37, 41–45)

THE ROOTS OF DISSENT

Once the Chairman had intervened to make His point, nobody on the board disputed it. On other occasions, however, questions were asked about the Chairman's style of management. Initially these occurred over simple matters, where Jesus' proposals seemed contrary to common sense—on catering, for instance:

Then he took [the disciples] with him and they withdrew by themselves to a town called Bethsaida, but the crowds learned about it and followed him. He welcomed them and spoke to them about the kingdom of God, and healed those who needed healing.

Late in the afternoon the Twelve came to him and said, "Send the crowd away so they can go to the surrounding villages and countryside and find food and lodging, because we are in a remote place here."

He replied, "You give them something to eat."

They answered, "We have only five loaves of bread and two fish—unless we go and buy food for all this crowd." (Luke 9:10–13)

It didn't make sense to the disciples that Jesus would do anything other than send the crowd away to restaurants and hotels. Their thinking wasn't broad enough to accommodate the idea that Jesus might make a few loaves and fish into a mass meal. And they showed the same literal-mindedness when confronted with the emerging "corporate policy." Thus, in John's version of the Last Supper—the last board meeting, if you like, before the Chairman's arrest—Jesus begins by outlining a distinctive code of behavior:

> *"My children, I will be with you only a little longer. You will look for me, and just as I told the Jews, so I tell you now: Where I am going, you cannot come.*
>
> *"A new command I give you: Love one another. As I have loved you, so you must love one another. By this all men will know that you are my disciples, if you love one another."* (John 13:33–35)

This is a key part of what we might describe as the corporation's "mission statement." (The other—and more literal—part of the mission statement comes at the end of Matthew [28:18–20], where Jesus tells His disciples to "go and make disciples of all nations.") Here in John 13, however, His mind has stuck on the earlier point:

> *Simon Peter asked him, "Lord, where are you going?"*
> *Jesus replied, "Where I am going, you cannot follow now, but you will follow later."*
> *Peter asked, "Lord, why can't I follow you now? I will lay down my life for you."* (verses 36–37)

He wouldn't, of course. But that's not the point. Evidently Peter thought that Jesus was about to go into hiding, in which case, it seemed to Peter, He might as well take Peter with Him. Later in the same meeting, Thomas still hadn't gotten the point: "Thomas said to him, 'Lord, we don't know where you are going, so how can we know the way?'" (John 14:5).

By this time, the suspicion had been growing among Jesus' board members that the whole thrust of the Chairman's policy was wrong. They had a great product, and many of them felt they should be maximizing its impact by taking it to a different market. In other words, they felt that Jesus should be cultivating support among the zealots, with a view to throwing off the yoke of Roman rule and becoming a political leader in His own right. The idea of Jesus opting for martyrdom had never gone down well in the boardroom:

> *From that time on Jesus began to explain to his disciples that he*

> *must go to Jerusalem and suffer many things at the hands of the elders, chief priests and teachers of the law, and that he must be killed and on the third day be raised to life.*
>
> *Peter took him aside and began to rebuke him. "Never, Lord!" he said. "This shall never happen to you!"*
>
> *Jesus turned and said to Peter, "Get behind me, Satan! You are a stumbling block to me; you do not have in mind the things of God, but the things of men." (Matthew 16:21–23)*

To be fair to Peter, this particular argument arose more out of his protectiveness than out of ideological opposition. The difference was fundamental—critical, even—but its roots lay in his ignorance and fear. Blind to God's wider purposes in the salvation of humankind, Peter could see no earthly point in Jesus getting Himself executed. And, understandably perhaps, he was afraid of what would happen to him once Jesus was dead. Having become so closely associated with Jesus' cause—having become, in fact, Jesus' right-hand man—Peter could hardly vanish into obscurity again as a Galilean fisherman.

Jesus' own board members, then, often misunderstood His objectives, misinterpreted His motives, and disagreed with His management style. They became frustrated and impatient with His sense of timing. And at times this underlying tension emerged in open dispute. If Jesus had been a little more democratic and a little less resolute, the Crucifixion and Resurrection would never have happened, and Jesus Himself would probably have been lost in the back pages of history as yet another failed Jewish revolutionary. But Jesus knew exactly where He wanted to take the corporation. And that meant that He had to deal with disagreement on a regular basis.

As the kind of person who often prays, "Lord, give me patience and do it now," I personally would find that constant attrition almost unbearable. It reminds me of the company president who, having crashed through his bottom line, called a staff meeting to explain that they were about to "go under." After the officers of the company had given all the figures and the president had summed up by saying that they could continue, at best, for only a few more weeks, an opportunity was given for questions. One dear lady raised her hand. Why, she wanted to know, wasn't the coffee wagon coming up to the thirteenth floor anymore?

To adopt the habit common in some big corporations of firing people who voice dissent or make mistakes is a prodigious waste of talent.

What intrigues me about Jesus, in view of the opposition He faced from inside His own camp, is why He didn't fire anyone. After all, He was very popular, particularly in the Galilean area. Given that John the Baptist had recently gone out of business—if that's not too glib a way to describe having his head chopped off—there would have been plenty of personnel available. Former executives in John's "company" would have been glad to join the Jesus team, and many did. Yet He didn't give Peter the pink slip even after Peter had questioned Jesus' deepest aims and Jesus had, in return, meted out to Peter the harshest rebuke recorded in the New Testament.

WORK WITH THE POTENTIAL

It's no coincidence that this rebuke to Peter comes hard on the heels of Jesus' recognition of Peter's representative faith as the rock—the linchpin—of the church. Despite his numerous and glaring faults, Peter had been chosen by Jesus to guide the infant church through its earliest and most formative years. Jesus saw the potential in Peter; he saw how Peter's bluff manner and natural charisma could, with a little thoughtfulness and restraint, be turned into just the sort of stuff to advance His mission.

It is true that ordinary folks like us do not have the benefit of Jesus' foresight and insight. Few of us can judge character and motivation with any kind of consistency. Nevertheless, the principle that holds for Jesus holds also for us. It's not what a person is now that matters—it's what he or she has the power to become. To adopt the habit common in some big corporations of firing people who voice dissent or make mistakes is a prodigious waste of talent. *Nobody* fits an organization 100 percent. The good people are the ones who learn from their mistakes and go on to perform better. Jesus outlines this philosophy in a parable:

> *"A man had a fig tree, planted in his vineyard, and he went to look for fruit on it, but did not find any. So he said to the man who took care of the vineyard, 'For three years now I've been coming to look for fruit on this fig tree and haven't found any. Cut it down! Why should it use up the soil?'*
>
> *"'Sir,' the man replied, 'leave it alone for one more year, and I'll dig around it and fertilize it. If it bears fruit next year, fine! If not, then cut it down.'"* (Luke 13:6–9)

Apply this thinking to the human resource policy in a corporation and two points come into focus. First, Jesus does not discount the possibility that the fig tree may in the end be uprooted and removed. The clear implication is that, since the fig tree uses up resources—just as an employee uses up a salary—it is reasonable for the vineyard owner to expect some return. But, second, this expectation, this demand, is balanced by a commitment to support and encourage. The fig tree is dug around and fertilized. In the same way, leaders in the corporate—and the religious—world are called on to give their juniors supervision, advice, training, and backup. We don't give up immediately on the person who refuses to follow the game plan. We are meant to be forgiving, in the sense that we leave the door open—as wide as we can and for as long as we can—for reconciliation and restoration.

I realize that this is a contentious issue. Leaders I know and respect have on occasion gently chided me for hanging on to a difficult employee when I should perhaps have let that person go long before. They consider me too magnanimous. Yet, if I'm going to err (and erring is, after all, human), I would rather err on the side of magnanimity.

That seems to me the burden of Jesus' teaching in this area.

JUDAS—A SPECIAL CASE?

A corporation needs a treasurer, and that was Judas's job. He carried the communal purse. The name *Iscariot* suggests that, unlike Jesus and the majority of the apostles, Judas came from the southern and more sophisticated part of the country—near the capital, Jerusalem. In the dispute John records between Judas and Jesus, Judas seems indeed to have taken a southerner's high-minded attitude toward the use of the group's funds:

> *Mary took about a pint of pure nard, an expensive perfume; she poured it on Jesus' feet and wiped his feet with her hair. And the house was filled with the fragrance of the perfume.*
>
> *But one of his disciples, Judas Iscariot, who was later to betray him, objected, "Why wasn't this perfume sold and the money given to the poor? It was worth a year's wages."* (John 12:3–5)

Judas wasn't the only one to think this way. Mark tells us that several people at the dinner expressed the same view (Mark 14:4). As a challenge to Jesus' own "corporate policy," this view had its merits: after all, a year's wages could go a long way toward helping a charitable cause. But though Judas appeared to eagerly seize this moral high ground, his real motive was very different: "He did not say this because he cared about the poor but because he was a thief; as keeper of the money bag, he used to help himself to what was put into it" (John 12:6).

Judas was an embezzler. He may have been other things too. People have come up with a good many suggestions as to why Judas decided to betray his Lord and Master, and it's certainly possible, as one person has said, that he had links to the Jewish zealots and went to the high priest in an attempt to force Jesus' hand in declaring Himself the Messiah. Whatever lay behind Judas's treachery, however, Jesus clearly had not brought him on board with the sole purpose of engineering His own arrest. The Bible implies that He chose Judas, just as He chose the other eleven disciples, for the potential the man possessed. Matthew says, "He called his twelve disciples to him and gave them authority to drive out evil spirits and to heal every disease and sickness" (Matthew 10:1). Named among those disciples is "Judas Iscariot, who betrayed him." (verse 4).

Did Jesus know from the very start what Judas would do? Of course. "Jesus had known from the beginning which of them did not believe and who would betray him" (John 6:64). Why, then, did Jesus not do what almost anyone else would have done, given this situation and this knowledge? The answer is obvious. Jesus knew not only that Judas would betray Him but that this miserable act would serve the Father's purpose.

In that respect, Jesus' treatment of Judas is special to Judas's case. We aren't called, as Christians, to suspend our critical faculties and let Satan demolish the work God is doing in our lives. Nevertheless, Judas represents those who come onto our boards or get elected to positions of leadership or join our staff but who know deep down that they have their own agenda. Of course, they will play along and declare that they've joined up out of passionate support for the institution's vision and mission, but from the start they believe that they can "improve" on the stated mission and expand the vision into something more spectacular. They want to change things. They want control.

In the past eighteen years I have hired two people like this in two different organizations. Despite my best efforts to be discerning, I was snookered into bringing people onto my team who had, from the outset, no intention of being team players. In both cases, when I confronted them, I found that their intention all along had been to "help bring change from within," while at the same time assenting to the organizational mission statement. To Christians in positions of responsibility, this kind of person poses a tough question.

DECIDING WHEN TO FIRE

The same question faced Paul the apostle. The whole letter of Galatians is an appeal to resist the subversive influence of certain false apostles who wished to promote the old Jewish belief that salvation could not be attained without circumcision. Paul, who himself had moved dramatically from Judaism into Christian faith, opposed this idea with all the strength he could muster.

He recalled an incident when the same issue had arisen. Fourteen years after his conversion Paul went up to Jerusalem to meet with the church leadership:

> *I went in response to a revelation and set before them the gospel that I preach among the Gentiles. But I did this privately to those who seemed to be leaders, for fear that I was running or had run my race in vain. Yet not even Titus, who was with me, was compelled to be circumcised, even though he was a Greek. This matter arose because some false brothers had infiltrated our ranks to spy on the freedom we have in Christ Jesus and to make us slaves. We did not give in to them for a moment, so that the truth of the gospel might remain with you. (Galatians 2:2–5)*

Later in the letter he got more specific:

> *Mark my words! I, Paul, tell you that if you let yourselves be circumcised, Christ will be of no value to you at all. Again I declare to every man who lets himself be circumcised that he is obligated to obey the whole law. You who are trying to be justified by law have been alienated from Christ; you have fallen away from grace. . . . The one who is throwing you into confusion will pay the penalty, whoever he may be. Brothers, if I am still preaching circumcision, why am I still being persecuted? In that case the offense of the cross has been abolished. As for those agitators, I wish they would go the whole way and emasculate themselves! (5:2–4,10–12)*

Paul could not effect the dismissal of the troublemakers because he was not physically present. But his attitude toward them and the principles on which he opposed them are clear from the nature of his writing.

First, he did not hesitate to identify the troublemakers as "false brothers." In other words, they had made their opposition to Paul's gospel abundantly clear, and on that basis he felt obliged to regard them as having forfeited their right of membership.

Second, these men were disturbing the peace of the church and the unity of the gospel message. Paul called them "agitators"; not content with being circumcised themselves, they were attempting to persuade the rest of the church to follow suit.

> *When debate slips into sedition and when*
> *private agendas are pushed to the point*
> *of subverting the overall mission, it is time*
> *for Christian leaders to take action.*

Third, Paul did not take the truth of his own position for granted. He went to some lengths at the beginning of the letter to lay out his credentials and emphasized that, when he went to Jerusalem to debate the issue of circumcision, he did so "privately to those who seemed to be leaders, for fear that I was running or had run my race in vain" (Galatians 2:2).

The fact that the leaders gave his gospel such a ringing endorsement explains why—fourth—he comes down so heavily against the dissidents. Unable to cut them off from the church, he expressed the wish that they would cut themselves off—in a more literal way!

The critical matter here seems to be that of damage to the organization. There is nothing wrong with diversity and debate. Jesus' own "board of directors" produced plenty of both. But when debate slips into sedition and when private agendas are pushed to the point of subverting the overall mission, it is time for Christian leaders to take action.

And yet firing, "letting go," is not the end. The purpose of all Christian action is, ultimately, the redemption of the lost. That is why we find a strange statement of Paul's in his first letter to Timothy:

> *Timothy, my son, I give you this instruction in keeping with the prophecies once made about you, so that by following them you may fight the good fight, holding on to faith and a good conscience. Some have rejected these and so have shipwrecked their faith. Among them are Hymenaeus and Alexander, whom I have handed over to Satan to be taught not to blaspheme. (1:18–20)*

Of Hymenaeus and Alexander we know almost nothing except what Paul told us here. It seems clear that their opposition forced Paul to relieve them of their responsibilities in God's corporation and to "let them go." But he did not kick the dust off his shoes and abandon them. He foresaw a time when they would realize the error of their ways. One day, he hoped, he'd have them back on the payroll.

9

PROGRESS:
The Life-Changer

"T hat man changed my life." Have you ever heard
someone say that? Maybe you can say it yourself.
Every now and again we come in contact with a person
who makes such a deep impression on us that we're never
the same again.

You don't have to meet the person face-to-face. Often it's
what the person has done, what he or she thinks or represents, that so powerfully impacts us. Talk to a Franciscan
friar about Francis of Assisi, or to a South African about
Nelson Mandela, or to almost anyone in the West about
Mother Teresa of Calcutta, and you'll see what I mean.

The strange thing is that almost none of these people—
the ones we know and the ones we don't—has set out to
change anyone's life. That occurred almost accidentally, as
a by-product of some quite different goal they aspired to
reach. Francis just wanted to build a church; Mandela
wanted justice in an unjust society; Mother Teresa intended
only to answer the call of God by ministering to the poor.

In the long run, people who *set out* to change lives nearly always fail. Look at the Soviet Union, where ideologues
struggled for decades to produce a socialist society in
which goods would be distributed, as Karl Marx had said,
"from each according to his ability to each according to his
need." But this high-sounding ideal soon crashed. From the
very start it relied on coercion, on making people do what

they didn't want, or only half-wanted, to do. In the end, the result wasn't a just society but a society dominated by inefficiency, relative poverty, and chronic dependence on the state.

The Soviet planners weren't the only ones who have tried to change people on a mass scale. Hitler wanted to change the world. So did Napoleon. So did all the leaders of major movements in history. I know, because such movements were the subject of my doctoral thesis. I looked in detail at how these movements were born, how they grew, and how they either died out or changed into something else. The study left me with one overriding conviction: No one has brought about change in the way Jesus brought about change.

CHANGE FROM THE INSIDE OUT

For one thing, Jesus worked from the inside out. To my knowledge, no leader who ever lived has changed people that way. Ideologues, despots, emperors, and dictators have sought to impose change *from the outside in*. In its crudest form, this involves winning obedience by intimidation: people do what's expected of them because, if they don't, they'll get a visit from the secret police. But even the subtlest exercises in propaganda and opinion management—and the methods used by Goebbels in Nazi Germany were fairly sophisticated—only work by hammering on people by appealing to fear and self-interest. Like television commercials, they can be persuasive, but they don't get you into the deepest part of another's personality. In the final analysis, these methods still rely on working inward from the outside. To work *from the inside out* you have to dispense with displays of power or appeals to self-interest or calls to ideological purity. You need something else. You need the power of example.

That was one of the main differences between, say, Abraham Lincoln and John F. Kennedy. Indisputably, both men were clever; both served their country well; both enjoyed enormous influence. Yet, at the end of the day, Lincoln tugs at our loyalty and affection in a way that JFK doesn't. Partly, no doubt, that's because we have no film footage of Lincoln, and his politics were uncontroversial enough to let him pass into that mythic realm reserved for great statesmen. But it's more than that. We sense also that Lincoln had the edge in being a fundamentally good and virtuous man. I say this with no disrespect to Kennedy, whose achievements were many. But if we had the choice of emulating one or the other, I think most of us would choose Lincoln.

That is true also of Francis of Assisi, Nelson Mandela, and Mother Teresa. They touch us deep inside, where part of us actually *wants* to become, in some respect, as good as they seem to be. And it's true also of Jesus—except far more so.

The Interview at the Well

Two chapters ago I began to tell the story of Jesus and the woman of Samaria. Their conversation starts when Jesus breaks with convention by asking the woman if she would pour Him a drink of water. If she knew who He was, Jesus goes on to say, she would have asked *Him* for "living water"—the life-giving Holy Spirit. "Sir," the woman said, "you have nothing to draw with and the well is deep. Where can you get this living water? Are you greater than our father Jacob, who gave us the well and drank from it himself, as did also his sons and his flocks and herds?" (John 4:11–12).

Jesus keeps bringing her back to the point:

> *He told her, "Go, call your husband and come back."*
> *"I have no husband," she replied.*
> *Jesus said to her, "You are right when you say you have no husband. The fact is, you have had five husbands, and the man you now have is not your husband. What you have just said is quite true."*
> *"Sir," the woman said, "I can see that you are a prophet."*
> *(verses 16–19)*

Jesus blocks this evasion by telling her, once again, that she had spoken the truth. He *is* a prophet—in fact, more than a prophet: the Messiah. "Then, leaving her water jar, the woman went back to the town and said to the people, 'Come, see a man who told me everything I ever did. Could this be the Christ?' They came out of the town and made their way toward him" (verses 28–30).

At first you might suppose that the Samaritan woman fancied herself an amateur theologian. But she showed little interest in theology. The controversies she tossed into the conversation—where the Messiah would come from, at which mountain God called His people to worship—were simply smoke screens to keep her personal life hidden. Yet she had so many pent-up longings (for forgiveness, for peace, for a fresh reputation) that once Jesus had won her trust she became a disciple instantaneously. Though she wouldn't have admitted as much, she was desperate. Her conversion seems to have happened almost as quickly as that of Saul of Tarsus, who was struck from his horse by a thunderbolt on the road to Damascus.

GOD'S TIMING

By contrast, the religious leader Nicodemus came into God's corporation rather more slowly.

> *Jesus answered, "I tell you the truth, no one can enter the kingdom of God unless he is born of water and the Spirit. Flesh gives birth to flesh, but the Spirit gives birth to spirit. You should not be surprised at my saying, 'You must be born again.' The wind blows wherever it pleases. You hear its sound, but you cannot tell where it comes from or where it is going. So it is with everyone born of the Spirit."*
>
> *"How can this be?" Nicodemus asked. (John 3:5–9)*

Unlike the woman of Samaria, Nicodemus was a genuine intellectual. He'd come to see Jesus because the reports about Him had tied his theology up in knots. His training told him that Jesus could not be the Messiah; yet, as he said in his opening gambit, "no one could perform the miraculous signs you are doing if God were not with him" (verse 2).

Jesus brings people into His corporation in very different ways.

Accepting Jesus' answer involved, for Nicodemus, not a release from the contradictions of his personal life but an intellectual paradigm shift—something that, by its very nature, does not happen overnight. In his book *Surprised by Joy*, C. S. Lewis pinpoints his conversion somewhere in the half hour it took him to travel on the bus from the center of Oxford to Headington. By the time he got off, he knew he'd stepped over the line into Christian faith. Yet for Lewis, as for Nicodemus, this moment capped a long, slow struggle to rearrange his ideas.

Not surprisingly, then, Nicodemus vanished from this encounter with Jesus without having made an explicit commitment. No sudden transformation here; Nicodemus didn't rush back to the Jewish ruling council crying, "He told me everything I ever did!" They would all have been in bed anyway, since he had come to see Jesus under cover of darkness.

It may be that the talk Jesus had with Nicodemus in John 3 was the first of many. What we do know is that a couple of years later Nicodemus reemerged a changed man—changed enough, at least, to take a great personal risk by helping Joseph of Arimathea take Jesus' body down from the cross and prepare it for burial (John 19:39–40).

Jesus brings people into His corporation in very different ways. Sometimes the process is painful. At other times it is exhilarating. Sometimes it is instantaneous; at other times, laborious. But He never uses the cookie-cutter approach of treating everyone the same way. People are different, with different needs, different emotional makeups, different situations. They will respond differently.

I know this not only as a pastor and leader but as the father of four children who are so different from each other that they could have come from four different planets. Every person is unique. No two individuals come into God's corporation by exactly the same route. God doesn't lump us together when we first arrive, nor does He treat us as anything less than complete individuals during all the changes that follow.

CHANGE IN TWO STAGES

A man was once admitted to the hospital for surgery. For weeks his wife had tried to make him see a doctor. Then, when he'd finally seen one, she tried for weeks to make him take the doctor seriously. He was a tough old guy who kept on insisting that there was nothing wrong with him that a good rest wouldn't fix. But finally the pain got so bad he couldn't ignore it anymore, and he agreed to go in for the operation.

Change in God's corporation comes in the same two stages. First, He changes our minds, then He changes our condition.

The doctor asked why he hadn't come in six months earlier. "Yeah, well," the man replied, "I didn't think I was really sick."

The doctor nodded. "Well," he said. "We've changed your mind. Now we're going to change your condition."

Change in God's corporation comes in the same two stages. First, He changes our minds, then He changes our condition. He wants—let me switch the metaphor—to give us on-the-job training. He wants to improve our skills and help us relearn and perform better. From start to finish, realizing that Jesus is in the executive suite involves change.

A Rock in a Hard Place?

Simon Peter's approach to life was *can-do*. He was Mr. Adequate, Mr. Self-confident—loud-mouthed, impulsive, proud, a leader by nature, not training. He had the ability to make decisions and bring others in behind him. What he lacked was perception, sensitivity, judgment, humility.

Then one day, while he was cleaning his nets, a stranger with a huge crowd of people in tow came up and asked if he could use Peter's boat as a podium.

> *When he had finished speaking, he said to Simon, "Put out into deep water, and let down the nets for a catch."*
>
> *Simon answered, "Master, we've worked hard all night and haven't caught anything. But because you say so, I will let down the nets."*
>
> *When they had done so, they caught such a large number of fish that their nets began to break. So they signaled their partners in the other boat to come and help them, and they came and filled both boats so full that they began to sink.*
>
> *When Simon Peter saw this, he fell at Jesus' knees and said, "Go away from me, Lord; I am a sinful man!" For he and all his companions were astonished at the catch of fish they had taken. (Luke 5:4–9)*

Let's update the story a little to appreciate its nuances. Peter runs a dealing floor, and his team is hard at work buying and selling stock when a preacher walks in. Peter has seen the guy on TV—in fact, he's speaking at a venue across the street. But it knocks him flat when the preacher comes up and tells him, "Put two million into such-and-such a bond." Peter looks at the preacher as though he's crazy. What does *He* know about stock trading? He walks into Peter's office, a man who's never even opened the *Wall Street Journal*, and tells Peter, one of the most experienced traders in the city, how to do his job! Peter feels like pointing this out, but something stops him. He swallows hard and tells an assistant to shift the funds. Five minutes later they've tripled in value.

This same lesson—that God can do better at what we're good at than we can—is hammered home with Peter again and again: Jesus calms a storm on the Lake of Galilee when Peter can't control the boat anymore; Jesus cuts sharply across Peter's apparently sensible plan to prevent the chief priests from arresting Him and having Him crucified; most dramatically, when Peter denies Jesus, Jesus turns and looks straight at him to bring to mind the apostle's empty bluster about never denying Him.

In many respects Peter's denial of Christ marked the turning point for Peter. It seemed to break his self-reliance. When, after the Resurrection, he took some of the other disciples down to Galilee to fish, it seemed as though he had come full circle:

> *Early in the morning, Jesus stood on the shore, but the disciples did not realize that it was Jesus.*
>
> *He called out to them, "Friends, haven't you any fish?"*
>
> *"No," they answered.*
>
> *He said, "Throw your net on the right side of the boat and you will find some." When they did, they were unable to haul the net in because of the large number of fish. (John 21:4–6)*

It's little wonder that Peter and the other disciples suddenly realized who this stranger was. The same message was being brought home by the same miracle. Peter could do nothing by himself. Even in the trade of which he was master, he was helpless without God's guidance. He had waited all night on the water and caught not so much as a minnow. This time, however, Peter seemed to get the message.

Immediately after the incident (see John 21:15–19), Jesus reinstated Peter's faith in Him as the "rock," the foundation for His church; and in the opening pages of Acts we see Peter emerging as a different person. Just a few weeks later, this simple fisherman, who had been too scared to declare his allegiance to Jesus, was standing up in Jerusalem and preaching God's word with supreme assurance. Coming into God's corporation had changed him forever.

The Man with Reservations

In complete contrast to Simon Peter was another disciple, Thomas. We often nickname him "Doubting Thomas." Yet I'm not sure that doubt lay at the root of Thomas's weakness. He was the kind of person who looks to the future and sees not possibilities but problems. There seems to have been something almost fatalistic in his discipleship, as though he knew right from the beginning that it would all go badly wrong. He would have watched with a sense of foreboding as opposition to Jesus gathered force in the south of the country, hoping against hope that Jesus would stay in the safety of the north; yet knowing also, as soon as the news of Lazarus's death came through, that the show-down in Jerusalem could not be avoided.

> *Then [Jesus] said to his disciples, "Let us go back to Judea."*
>
> *"But Rabbi," they said, "a short while ago the Jews tried to stone you, and yet you are going back there?"...*
>
> *So then he told them plainly, "Lazarus is dead, and for your sake I am glad I was not there, so that you may believe. But let us go to him." (John 11:7–8, 14–15)*

With the bad news confirmed, Thomas resolutely bit the bullet: "Then Thomas (called Didymus) said to the rest of the disciples, 'Let us also go, that we may die with him'" (verse 16).

Like the others, Thomas consistently misunderstood the nature of Jesus' mission. He didn't criticize Jesus openly; he just couldn't make sense of it all. Jesus told him, "If I go and prepare a place for you, I will come back and take you to be with me that you also may be where I am. You know the way to the place where I am going" (John 14:3–4). Thomas immediately replied, "Lord, we don't know where you are going, so how can we know the way?" (verse 5).

The arrest came in Gethsemane, followed by the cruci-fixion, and the weight of Thomas's accumulated pessimism collapsed on him. While the other disciples prattled about Jesus coming back to life, Thomas remained steadfastly and comfortlessly realistic: Jesus was dead, and dead people didn't rise. "Now Thomas (called Didymus), one of the Twelve, was not with the disciples when Jesus came" (John 20:24). When the other disciples told him that they had seen the Lord, he declared, "Unless I see the nail marks in his hands and put my finger where the nails were, and put my hand into his side, I will not believe it" (verse 25). He was in for a famous surprise:

A week later his disciples were in the house again, and Thomas was with them. Though the doors were locked, Jesus came and stood among them and said, "Peace be with you!" Then he said to Thomas, "Put your finger here; see my hands. Reach out your hand and put it into my side. Stop doubting and believe."

Thomas said to him, "My Lord and my God!" (verses 26–28)

Those five words mark Thomas's release into the true liberty of faith. Jesus the life-changer had touched him and brought him a new kind of realism—the realism of the Resurrection. For all of us, Jesus is the life-changer. He changes us by bringing us into His corporation—the call of a lifetime—and then once we're in it He goes on working to bring us to the limits of our potential. He does it in different ways. The training program is suited to our own individual needs and temperaments. The change He brought about in Peter was different from the one He brought about in Thomas. And both are different from the change He is working in me and in you. But when Jesus sits in the executive suite, things change. He makes them change. And they change for good.

10

ISOLATION:
It's Lonely at the Top

He looked me in the eye after I had made a major decision in my life and said, "It's true, you know."
I asked, "What is true?"
"It's lonely at the top."
Until that moment I hadn't fully comprehended the phrase. It was a cliché, something people said without thinking. But now, suddenly, it had meaning for me. My friend was a corporate executive of many years, and he understood the loneliness that comes from making the right decision on the basis, not of other people's advice, but of your own inner conviction.

Loneliness is the price of initiative. Some people choose that initiative because they form their own organizations or get promoted to the top. Others have it thrust upon them when they are forced to stand up for their principles or find themselves at the head of a team without adequate backup.

However it happens, you're likely to experience loneliness. Suddenly you find there's nobody else who sees things from quite the angle you see them. Those you might get support from seem to be sitting someplace else: they don't understand. You have people around you (more people, perhaps, than ever before), yet in a profound sense you're on your own.

THE ELIJAH SYNDROME

This loneliness is a two-edged sword. On the one hand, it can keep you away from distractions. If you're the only one who can make a decision, that very knowledge can aid your powers of concentration. You know for a certainty that it all depends on you. And there is no doubt that God uses men and women who disregard well-meaning advice and cut their own path. On the other hand, the loneliness of initiative carries a number of costs:

- *You* take the rap for any mistakes.
- Those under you may be quick to resent any decisions that affect them adversely.
- All the people you work with become your "followers" or "employees," not your equals and friends.
- You may have to maintain the appearance of strength, even when you feel like giving up.
- You very seldom get thanked.

Worse than any of this, you may begin to develop the Elijah syndrome. This is a deep-rooted and nagging suspicion that the stand you've taken is opposed by practically everybody else in the world and that, consequently, you may as well give up.

God called on the prophet Elijah to take the initiative against the false religion of Baal that was wreaking havoc in Israel. At first, and with memorable bravado, Elijah lays into his enemies like a gunslinging marshal in an out-of-control Wild West saloon: "Ahab went to meet Elijah. When he saw Elijah, he said to him, 'Is that you, you troubler of Israel?' 'I have not made trouble for Israel,' Elijah replied. 'But you and your father's family have. You have abandoned the Lord's commands and have followed the Baals'" (1 Kings 18:16–18).

Elijah proceeds to throw down the gauntlet to King Ahab. He proposes a contest on Mount Carmel between himself and the 450 prophets of Baal. Two sacrifices are to be prepared; whichever of the gods burned up his sacrifice first would be declared the winner. It was as close as the

Old Testament comes to a heavyweight title fight, and Elijah was looking for a knockout. When the prophets of Baal fail to rouse their god, Elijah begins to taunt them, so they try even harder (1 Kings 18:27–28).

Nothing happens. To add insult to injury, Elijah commands that his own altar be doused three times with water (verses 33–35). He steps forward and prays for God to let the fire fall, and it does, licking up not only the wood and the sacrifice, but also the soil and the water in the surrounding trench. Completing the victory, Elijah orders the people to slaughter all the prophets of Baal (verses 36–40). King Ahab returns to Jezreel to relay the news to his wife Jezebel. The result?

> *Jezebel sent a messenger to Elijah to say, "May the gods deal with me, be it ever so severely, if by this time tomorrow I do not make your life like that of one of them."*
>
> *Elijah was afraid and ran for his life. When he came to Beersheba in Judah, he left his servant there, while he himself went a day's journey into the desert. He came to a broom tree, sat down under it and prayed that he might die. (1 Kings 19:2–4)*

Mount Carmel Today?

Probably most of us have some experience of being the odd one out, feeling that we don't belong, of receiving from others not support but criticism. The frequency with which we face this kind of situation makes it all the more important to distinguish loneliness from the Elijah syndrome and to prevent ourselves sliding from one into the other.

In 1991 the church that I pastor was named among the fastest-growing congregations in its denomination. Soon after this a dispute arose in that denomination, and we felt compelled to take a stand. It was a stand for biblical morality in a church tradition where the clergy, in particular, have increasingly drifted from orthodox faith. This failure among the clergy was one reason we made the tough decision to mobilize the laity. It is no secret that in most mainline denominations like ours the laity is far more orthodox than the clergy.

Pity parties aren't supposed to go on indefinitely. Sooner or later everybody's got to pack up and get on with their lives.

That seemed to be the trigger. Soon I found myself on the receiving end of a torrent of abusive letters and phone calls. Did I get support from any of my fellow ministers? Not one. In fact, even my friends deserted me. They all seemed to assume that I'd dug in my heels out of arrogance. The kindest letter said, "I'm sorry you're under attack, but you really brought it upon yourself!"

I guess Elijah's friends might have said the same thing. For the next several weeks I experienced some of the loneliest moments in my ministry. I began to understand what Elijah felt like—being left high and dry with nobody to keep me company. Then the Lord led me to a small group of pastors in the city who, though not of my denomination, shared my convictions and felt, if anything, more strongly than I did. Along with a core of godly lay leaders in my own congregation, these men supported me through the battle and kept me from sliding into the sort of mental cellar Elijah reached after defeating the prophets of Baal.

Three Reasons to Avoid the Elijah Syndrome

Nobody likes getting a death threat, as Elijah did. But the Elijah syndrome can take over for far less dramatic reasons than that, and there are good reasons for staying clear of it.

1. It prolongs the pity party. One of the most common human responses to hardship is self-pity. Something goes wrong, and we hold a pity party. Often we invite our friends so everybody can sit around and agree what a rotten time we've had. It's a psychological survival trick, something to help us over the tough times.

But there's a danger. Pity parties aren't supposed to go on indefinitely. Sooner or later everybody's got to pack up and get on with their lives. Staying in a state of self-pity not only leads to a form of idolatry (an obsession with your own welfare) but stops you from tackling the real issues underlying your situation. Moaning at God might have made Elijah feel better, but it wasn't going to stop Jezebel from turning him into dog food. He needed to act. And if there's one thing pity parties stop us from doing, it's taking action. Instead, we keep on affirming to ourselves that we are victims of circumstance and reinforcing a frame of mind in which resistance seems pointless.

2. *It distorts your perception.* It's that closed circle of reasoning ("me and the problem I can't overcome") that stops us from seeing the way forward. In Elijah's case, you can see the seeds of it already present in his attitude before the contest at Mount Carmel. Not long before he confronted Ahab, he'd been reminded of Obadiah's faithfulness in preserving a hundred prophets from assassination (see 1 Kings 18:13). Yet, when he stood up to address the crowd at Mount Carmel, he'd already got it firmly in his head that he was the last of God's men left in the field. At the time, perhaps, the thought helped to motivate him. But shortly afterward, with Jezebel's death squads on his tail, the implications of his loneliness began to dawn on him. If he really *was* the last man out there, his time would soon be up.

But, of course, he wasn't the last man. As God told him, "I reserve seven thousand in Israel—all whose knees have not bowed down to Baal and all whose mouths have not kissed him" (1 Kings 19:18). Until God shook him out of his depression, Elijah couldn't—or wouldn't—admit it. Yet the support of those seven thousand snapped the spell. When he heard about them, he immediately took action.

3. *It deprives others of your support.* There is a certain arrogance in thinking that you're the only one left manning the stockade. But believe it or not, God is too smart to let His purposes rest on your performance alone. Whatever kind of isolation you find yourself in, if you look around long enough, you will find others who feel the same way.

The *feeling* that it's lonely at the top seldom accords with the reality. And, more likely than not, those others will feel just as much in need of support and understanding as you do. By refusing to acknowledge them, therefore, you cut them off from the assistance you might have supplied. You develop a victim consciousness. You think you need to be helped. And yet the way forward isn't to lie groaning on your own stretcher but to pick up someone else's.

The first thing Elijah did was seek out one of the seven thousand—Elisha, his successor—and take him on as an assistant. It was a positive move, one that made a connection between two isolated people and made both stronger as a result.

The Loneliness of Jesus

Theologians have sometimes said that it was God's desire to relate to another person outside Himself that led Him to create the human race. That may or may not be true. But it's hard to imagine anyone closer to the top than God, and if it's lonely at the top, there must be a special kind of loneliness associated with the heavenly throne.

For Jesus, then, loneliness had a double edge: not only did His divine nature isolate Him from His parents and peers, on top of that His human nature in some sense isolated Him from God. Why else, as a boy, did He feel drawn to stay in His Father's house—the temple at Jerusalem—long after Mary and Joseph and the rest of the party had gone home?

On both sides the loneliness seemed to deepen with time. His neighbors refused to take Him seriously. His closest friends consistently failed to understand His mission. The religious and political authorities of the day were united in vehement opposition to His teaching. His most trusted friend and colleague abandoned Him at His trial and denied any association with Him. He had no possessions, no property, no security, no ordinary work. Even His grave was borrowed.

Jesus felt these rejections just as sharply as we would have. He knows what it's like to be isolated. In addition, He experienced not only the separation from God that is implicit in His taking human form; He also suffered the outright rejection of God that resulted from carrying humanity's sin to the cross. We cannot imagine, any more than the disciples did, what kind of anguish Jesus went through at that period. No wonder the prophet Isaiah, looking forward to Christ's coming, saw Him as "despised and rejected by men, a man of sorrows, and familiar with suffering. Like one from whom men hide their faces he was despised" (Isaiah 53:3).

> *If you put your membership in God's corporation before everything else, you can expect every now and again to run into conflicts of loyalty.*

Despite all that, however, the Gospels never once show Jesus pitying Himself. He did not succumb to the Elijah syndrome. Rather, He made His acceptance of loneliness a pattern for all who would come after.

Next time a colleague or friend or loved one sells you out for a small fee, remember that Jesus stood where you are. Next time you see the ideals for which you stand trampled underfoot by others, remember that Jesus stood where you are. Next time those you most rely on withdraw their public support, remember that Jesus stood where you are. For Christians, loneliness isn't always a calamity to be shunned. In many ways it comes with the territory.

HOW TO BE LONELY

As a Christian you are set apart just by the nature of your priorities. Not that those priorities should make you unappetizingly pious, but if you put your membership in God's corporation before everything else, you can expect every now and again to run into conflicts of loyalty. Unexpectedly, you may be vulnerable to hostile criticism, resentment, and ridicule. When you face that kind of loneliness, it's worth keeping two things in mind.

1. Standing on your own builds strength of character. It's no coincidence that Jesus went alone into the desert for the temptations. Nor, I think, is it a coincidence that Joseph's abilities as an administrator blossomed in situations where he was, in the cultural and religious sense, cut off from his roots. Despite being a stranger in a strange land, he brought such prosperity to his master Potiphar's house that "with Joseph in charge, [Potiphar] did not concern himself with anything except the food he ate" (Genesis 39:6). Likewise, after Potiphar's wife denounced Joseph and he was thrown into prison, "he was made responsible for all that was done there. The warden paid no attention to anything under Joseph's care, because the Lord was with Joseph and gave him success in whatever he did" (verses 22–23).

2. You're never alone. At the time God called me to make a stand for biblical orthodoxy in my denomination, I felt, despite the lack of support from my fellow clergy, a particularly strong sense of God's presence. Times of loneliness with respect to others are often the times of most perfect intimacy with the Father. When I cannot express my passion for the lost even to my nearest and dearest, my relationship with God seems to deepen beyond measure.

Read our mission statement as outlined by Jesus: "Therefore go and make disciples of all nations, baptizing them in the name of the Father and of the Son and of the Holy Spirit, and teaching them to obey everything I have commanded you" (Matthew 28:19–20). Jesus goes on to make the promise that no other faith has replicated: "And surely I am with you always, to the very end of the age" (verse 20). There is no isolation for us of the kind that Jesus Himself endured. We are never cut off from God. "Who shall separate us from the love of Christ?" (Romans 8:35). The answer is no one. No one has the power. And the one person who *does* have the power— Jesus Himself—is our friend and advocate. In our loneliness, therefore, we are always in His presence.

WHEN LONELINESS IS SOMETHING ELSE

Sometimes there's more to loneliness than meets the eye. Moses entered into a leadership position unwillingly.

After God had stopped him at the burning bush, giving him a commission to deliver the Israelites from Egypt and equipping him with a battery of devastating miraculous powers, Moses replied, "O Lord, please send someone else to do it" (Exodus 4:13).

Although God reluctantly allowed Aaron, Moses' brother, to make up what Moses lacked as a public speaker, Moses continued to feel isolated and vulnerable. Also, the nature of his leadership responsibilities changed. Representing the people before Pharaoh and taking them through the Red Sea was one thing; keeping an entire nation fed and watered in a forty-year trek across Sinai was quite another. Moses seems to have had little flair for logistics. Consequently, any losses from his immediate staff were deeply unsettling for him:

> *Now Moses said to Hobab son of Reuel the Midianite, Moses' father-in-law, "We are setting out for the place about which the Lord said, 'I will give it to you.' Come with us and we will treat you well, for the Lord has promised good things to Israel."*
>
> *He answered, "No, I will not go; I am going back to my own land and my own people."*
>
> *But Moses said, "Please do not leave us. You know where we should camp in the desert, and you can be our eyes. If you come with us, we will share with you whatever good things the Lord gives us." (Numbers 10:29–32)*

This passage—not one of the best-known in the Old Testament—is highly revealing. It shows the extent of Moses' responsibilities and how he tried to relieve the pressure of leadership by off-loading some of these responsibilities onto others. Hobab was an adviser he could ill-afford to lose, and Hobab's departure may explain why, a little later on, the pressures on Moses reached the boiling point:

> *Moses heard the people of every family wailing, each at the entrance to his tent. The Lord became exceedingly angry, and Moses was troubled. He asked the Lord, "Why have you brought this trouble on your servant? What have I done to displease you that*

you put the burden of all these people on me? Did I conceive all these people? Did I give them birth? Why do you tell me to carry them in my arms, as a nurse carries an infant, to the land you promised on oath to their forefathers? Where can I get meat for all these people? They keep wailing to me, 'Give us meat to eat!' I cannot carry all these people by myself; the burden is too heavy for me." (Numbers 11:10–14)

Perhaps Moses should have released some of this tension before he exploded in God's presence. Nevertheless, the answer to the problem, as God's response shows, is to spread the load. Seventy elders of Israel were chosen to share the burden with Moses. They were not his equals, but God put on them the same Spirit he put on Moses. In that way He multiplied Moses' presence in the camp and made it easier for him to impose his authority.

For Moses, then, loneliness was not simply a matter of strain brought about by isolation—though the only people he seems able to relate to as equals were members of his own family (see, for instance, his encounter with Jethro in Exodus 18:13–26). Tied up with his loneliness was an organizational problem. He had too much routine responsibility. To function optimally he needed first to delegate (as he did on Jethro's advice) his work as a magistrate and later to share his leadership authority with a group of men who became elders.

The lesson? If you feel lonely in your work, look first at the way your responsibilities connect you to, or cut you off from, other people. Under Jesus' leadership you're not expected to be an all-singing, all-dancing solo performer. In God's corporation, your links to other people are given a high value. It's worth cultivating them.

11

PRAYER:
Plugged in at the Source

I once heard a story about a widowed father who had only one child—a daughter who loved him dearly. They often spent time together, sometimes simply walking in silence or gazing at hills and trees. But one day the girl declined her father's invitation to walk. "I am sorry," she said, "I have something urgent to do." The next day she said the same thing. And the next.

Time after time for weeks the father would invite her to join him. "Come walk with me," he'd say. "Let's see the new flowers in bloom." And each time she had an excuse for declining.

Finally the father said to her, "Please walk with me today. It's my birthday." This time the girl said yes. But first she asked him to wait. She raced to her room and returned with a package neatly wrapped. She beamed as he opened it. Inside was a pair of beautiful, hand-sewn slippers. She'd spent weeks working on them. They were perfect. Exquisite.

"Thank you," her father said with tears in his eyes.

"Do you understand now, Father, why I couldn't walk with you for the past several weeks? I was making the slippers for you."

He thanked her again, and they went for their walk, both of them remarking how much they had missed one another's company. Finally, the father said, "Darling, I love the slippers. They are beautiful, and it touches me deeply that you put so much work into them." But there was a pensive note in his voice.

His daughter immediately picked this up, and asked, "What's wrong, Father?"

He hesitated, then said, "As much as I appreciate the slippers, I would rather have bought them, no matter what the price. For over these past weeks I've been robbed of something far more valuable—your companionship."

WHAT KIND OF WORK ETHIC?

Was the father ungrateful? I don't think so. He was speaking the truth. And if we listen carefully for the voice of God, many of us will hear something similar. "You love Me, you want to serve Me, and you show this by working extremely hard. I am glad for what you are doing in My name. But I would rather have your company than your work."

Does that go against the grain? Our culture—including our Christian culture—tells us that hard work is commendable. *Not* working, by contrast, is seen either as a misfortune visited on us by injury or unemployment or as a flaw resulting from downright laziness. How many of us pay more than lip service to the idea that spending time with God matters more than working for Him? Instinct tells us the opposite. A person, we tell ourselves, can be so heavenly minded as to be of no earthly use.

> *In a fast-moving world, prayer
> soon tumbles down the agenda.*

It was a fond habit of the old Soviet government to paste up posters inciting the workforce to greater productivity. Americans need no such encouragement. From our earliest days we are brought up on a diet of goal-driven activism. Doing is everything. Getting results is everything. Dedication is everything. And the result is that, like the young lawyer I mentioned in my introduction, whose boss regarded twelve hours as a "half day," we will throw ourselves into the stiffest of challenges just to prove that we can do it. All it takes is for someone to show us a target, and we charge at it like a bull at a red rag.

In this kind of atmosphere, time spent with God isn't exactly frowned on, but it is devalued. Reared on activity, we're unable to believe that an hour on our knees is an hour well spent. Occasionally we see prayer as an investment—when we want, for instance, to land a new job or receive healing from cancer. But even at these times the impetus soon runs out, and we're reluctant to allocate to our prayer any more than the day's leftover minutes. In a fast-moving world, prayer soon tumbles down the agenda. Yet prayer is a work issue in two important ways.

First, work *needs* prayer. Contrary to the popular saying, the act of working isn't itself a form of prayer. But work involves far-reaching decisions and the management of crucial relationships, and so demands all the divine help and inspiration we can get. It was Martin Luther who said, "I have so much to do that I must spend the first three hours of each day in prayer."

Second, though, and paradoxically, prayer and employment often make a poor marriage. That prayer plays second fiddle to *pleasure* is self-evident: sitting, after all, is more comfortable than kneeling, and watching a movie takes less effort than intercession. So you might think that compared to clocking in at the factory, prayer comes off rather well. But it doesn't. And the reason isn't so much that people enjoy their work (frequently they don't) but that the work serves a tangible purpose that prayer, apparently, does not. Who, we ask, can afford the luxury of prayer when there's a mortgage to pay, a job to hold on to, children to feed, a family Christmas to pay for?

DOUBLE-THINK PRAYER

When it comes to praying, then, the church seems not to know its right hand from its left. On Sunday, everyone nods in agreement when the pastor tells them how much more they need to pray. But on Monday, everyone—including the pastor—starts working in a way that puts prayer firmly on the margins. I know because I've done it myself.

Immediately after we founded the Church of the Apostles in 1987, new people were coming in droves. They all wanted to meet the pastor, and the pastor wanted to meet them. But because most of them were businesspeople, the meetings had to take place outside office hours; consequently, I began logging my calendar, days in advance, with 7:00 A.M. breakfasts, noon lunches, and 7:00 P.M. dinners. That, of course, was in addition to all my other appointments.

I felt totally comfortable about this. After all, if I was going to be "successful" as a pastor, I had to be available, to be seen, to be on top of things. Little did I know I was playing right into the Devil's hands. He had me running ragged, and gradually my early morning prayer and devotions began to suffer.

One day I tried to get out of bed early as usual, but I felt so tired I changed my mind and decided to sleep in. It didn't help. By midday I knew there was something wrong. I looked at my bulging calendar, knowing I had to ditch some of the appointments but reluctant to admit to myself I was anything less than indestructible. In the end, I was forced to cancel a whole block of my schedule, for I had contracted double pneumonia.

It was like being paralyzed. I couldn't read. I couldn't do anything. Only after two days did it occur to me that this forced inactivity might be a blessing. After all, the one thing I *could* still do was pray. I resolved to spend my waking hours in prayer. I don't mean twenty or thirty minutes (in spite of the pressure I'd managed to keep that much going)—I mean whole slabs of time devoted to communing with my heavenly Father, pouring my heart out to Him, interceding, weeping, and hearing His sweet voice.

He said this to me: "Now that I have your attention, I want to tell you a few things. Chief among them: you have fallen into the trap of believing that you can meet people's needs and do everything else you do by your own effort."

I wept bitterly, asking for the Lord's forgiveness. Suffice

it to say, I seldom now make a breakfast appointment. That first part of the day is the Lord's—and the Lord's alone! The lesson was so simple I can barely believe I needed to learn it. But I did. And when I hear today that the average American evangelical pastor spends less than twenty minutes in prayer every day, whereas the average Korean pastor spends ninety minutes, I'm not surprised at what God is doing in Korea.

WORK OR WORTH?

What's behind our obsession with "doing"? Here is where I see the problem: we muddle up work and worth. Despite all the books, tapes, lectures, and sermons Christians absorb in an effort to feel better about themselves, many struggle with a poor self-image. Deep inside they believe that, if only they could work a little harder and produce a little more, they would find greater acceptance with their fellow believers and with God. It's the Protestant work ethic gone into over-drive. Not only are they positively motivated to work, but they can't slow down. They work to achieve worth. In the midst of this, four basic biblical truths get lost:

1. Each of us is fully loved right now.
2. Each of us is totally acceptable to God as we are right now.
3. We can do nothing to make God love us more.
4. We can do nothing to make God love us less.

In light of these truths, look again at the familiar story of Mary and Martha:

> *As Jesus and his disciples were on their way, he came to a village where a woman named Martha opened her home to him. She had a sister called Mary, who sat at the Lord's feet listening to what he said. But Martha was distracted by all the preparations that had to be made. She came to him and asked, "Lord, don't you care that my sister has left me to do the work by myself? Tell her to help me!"*

> *"Martha, Martha,"* the Lord answered, *"you are worried and upset about many things, but only one thing is needed. Mary has chosen what is better, and it will not be taken away from her."* (Luke 10:38–42)

Notice that the story is *not* about being loved by God or being acceptable to God. Mary and Martha were both loved and accepted. Nothing they did—laboring or listening—could make Jesus love them more or less. They didn't need to prove anything. Yet the arrival of Jesus in their home provoked contrasting reactions. Mary was content to sit and listen, whereas Martha—no doubt fearing the scandal of an unlaid table or an undercooked roast—fretted about the practicalities involved in preparing Jesus His dinner.

In my view, Martha didn't understand that Jesus' love for her was unconditional, that it didn't depend on her performance in the kitchen. That was the "better part," which Mary had and Martha lacked. Mary was confident enough of God's love that she was able to put work aside. In fact, she *wanted* to spend time with Jesus. Her worth didn't depend on her work. For Martha, on the other hand, the bottom line was defined not by the all-important presence of Jesus but by the need to meet a certain standard of catering. If she failed that test, she felt, her ratings with Jesus would fall.

BE NOW, DO LATER?

Anyone who's had the experience of cooking for guests will say, "Well, that's fine, but in the end somebody's got to cook, or there won't be a meal!" That's right. The work matters. At no point did Jesus imply that the cooking didn't need doing, or even that Martha shouldn't be doing it. Similarly for Christians, the choice between work and prayer is not one between good and bad but between good and better. Without the "better" of prayer, work itself loses meaning.

We have to "be" as well as "do," and what we *do*—in our families, churches, and places of work—derives its significance from what we *are* as those who have received the call of a lifetime. Martha wasn't just a sous-chef sweating away in a basement kitchen; she was a woman who had "opened her home" to Jesus. That fact bestowed on her a natural dignity and honor.

In the Westminster Shorter Catechism, the first question and answer reads, "Q. 1. What is the chief end of man? A. Man's chief end is to glorify God, and to enjoy Him for ever." That is what is meant by being plugged in at the source. That's what we're here for. It is, if you like, the reason behind God's corporate mission statement, the Great Commission. In order to achieve the glorification and enjoyment of God, we are to bring to God as many of our fellow men, women, and children as we can.

Prayer and work, then, become subjects of prioritization. God wants us to serve others. He wants us to share the gospel, care for the sick and dying, use our gifts. All these tasks are important. So too is the daily work by which we earn money and support ourselves and our families. Paul, after all, set a characteristically firm example here:

> We were not idle when we were with you, nor did we eat anyone's food without paying for it. On the contrary, we worked night and day, laboring and toiling so that we would not be a burden to any of you. We did this, not because we do not have the right to such help, but in order to make ourselves a model for you to follow. For even when we were with you, we gave you this rule, "If a man will not work, he shall not eat." (2 Thessalonians 3:7–10)

This warning against idleness and the reminder of Paul's daylong labor were written in a letter that Paul began with the assurance, "we constantly pray for you" (1:11). No work, in other words, is to come before our relationship with God. No matter how packed our schedule, how heavy our workload, we need to have our spiritual tanks refilled daily before we can operate at our best.

"My first job is serving Jesus."
—James L. Kraft, founder of Kraft Foods

Jesus set an example in this as well. Imagine that Jesus had used a Daytimer and that an archaeologist dug it up, perfectly preserved. I'm convinced that the first line of every day would read something like this: "Spending time with My Father." To be sure, Jesus spoke often about His active ministry: "doing the will of the Father," "fulfilling all righteousness," "obeying the Father," and so on. Yet these callings never conflicted with His prayer. Repeatedly Jesus made time in a hectic day to be on His own with God. He needed that. And if *He* needed it, so do we. When the plug comes loose, we lose power.

TALK TO THE CHAIRMAN

When he was a young man, James L. Kraft, founder of Kraft Foods, wanted to be the most famous manufacturer and salesman of cheese in the world. This ambition saw humble beginnings. He made the cheese himself, loaded it onto a small wagon, and went around the streets of Chicago with Paddy, his pony, trying to sell it. Months went by. He worked his hands to the bone. But, despite this colossal commitment of time and energy, he was making hardly anything.

One day he pulled his pony to a stop and began to talk to him. "Paddy," he said, "something's wrong. We're not doing it right. I'm afraid we have things turned around, and we've put our priorities in the wrong place. Maybe we ought to serve God and place Him first in our lives."

What the pony made of this we shall never know. But as soon as he got home, Kraft made a covenant that, for the rest of his life, he would serve God first and then work as God directed. Many years later, his ambition realized, he was heard to say this: "I would rather be a layman in my church than to head the greatest corporation in America. My first job is serving Jesus."

Kraft understood the two corporations I spoke of at the beginning of this book. He knew that both were important. And he knew that to work properly in his worldly corporation he had to recognize, and submit to, the leadership of the heavenly one. "My first job is serving Jesus." That says it all.

But how can we serve Jesus if we don't make time for prayer? Prayer marks our attendance at the corporate management meeting. It connects us to what's going on. It inspires us, motivates us, informs us, empowers us. Without it, we're out of touch.

I know from my own experience that prayer bridges the gap between perceived and real effectiveness. Much haste, after all, can make little speed. When I am plugged into the source, I can accomplish more in two hours than I can otherwise accomplish in two weeks. Why? Because I am doing the corporation's work under the direct instruction of the corporation's Chairman.

In God's corporation, you see, there is an intimacy you will never find in a human organization. At the center of everything stands the believer's relationship with Christ— not a job description, not a mission statement, not an eternal pension scheme, but a relationship. And that relationship is itself far closer than any relationship you will find between managers or workers. It's more like a marriage.

Marriage is the closest analogy and provides us with some clues as to how to maintain the relationship well. For instance, we realize today how important communication is to marriage. My wife of twenty-four years, who is my best friend, will tell you that communication means spending time together. Starved of interaction, communication breaks down, and the marriage begins to fall apart. It's only common sense. Yet how many Christians apply this common sense to their spiritual lives? Do they seriously expect to develop a relationship with God if they won't talk to Him or let Him talk to them?

I know this isn't easy. As a friend of mine once said, whenever you start to pray, the doorbell rings, the phone rings, the roof leaks, the cat meows, the dog barks. We are naive if we think that Satan doesn't have an interest in derailing our prayer. Satan runs a competing company. He's after God's market share, and he will stop at nothing to sow discord in God's management. This is a key strategy for him because God trains us to an extraordinarily high standard. The intimacy we have with the Chairman enables us to come clean and confess our shortcomings. In acknowledging our dependence on Him and His authority over us, we allow ourselves to be cleansed and forgiven and made more effective for God's service. In other words, if you're praying, Satan won't be sitting on his hands waiting for you to finish.

But persevere. Prayer is the point at which our membership in God's corporation becomes real. It is also the means through which we maintain our relationship with God and thus renew our effectiveness for the gospel. And as Kraft found out, the discipline it imposes on our priorities spreads out to influence every part of our lives.

So if you want to work for God—that is, if you want your daily work to be a *Christian* activity, a part of your discipleship—begin by talking to the Chairman. Seek His power to resist the influence of the satanic competition. Give praise and adoration to God and His Son Jesus Christ. Use your time with Him for self-examination, confession, and repentance. Intercede for your family, for your church, and—of course—for your work.

The business belongs to God. All business does. One day, if you are faithful to the aims of God's corporation, you will be given a heavenly promotion that makes the chairmanship of a multinational corporation look like being head cheerleader in high school. In the long term it is God's plan, through Jesus, to bring you to the executive suite you've never seen—the executive suite from which the universe itself is run. "Well done, good and faithful servant!" (Matthew 25:21). That's a promotion worth working for.